THE *Barefoot* BINGO CALLER

A MEMOIR

Antanas Sileika

Published by ECW Press
665 Gerrard Street East,
Toronto, Ontario, Canada M4M 1Y2
416-694-3348 / info@ecwpress.com

LIBRARY AND ARCHIVES CANADA
CATALOGUING IN PUBLICATION

Sileika, Antanas, 1953-, author
The barefoot bingo caller : a memoir / Antanas Sileika.

Issued in print and electronic formats.
ISBN 978-1-77041-342-9 (paperback)
ISBN 978-1-77305-024-9 (pdf)
ISBN 978-1-77305-023-2 (epub)

1. Sileika, Antanas, 1953-. 2. Authors, Canadian (English)—20th century—Biography. I. Title.

PS8587.I2656Z46 2017   C813'.54   C2016-906390-9
C2016-906391-7

Cover design: Michel Vrana
Cover images: © Charles Taylor/iStockPhoto
Type: Rachel Ironstone
Inside cover photos: Courtesy Antanas Sileika

The publication of *The Barefoot Bingo Caller* has been generously supported by the Canada Council for the Arts, which last year invested $153 million to bring the arts to Canadians throughout the country, and by the Government of Canada through the Canada Book Fund. *Nous remercions le Conseil des arts du Canada de son soutien. L'an dernier, le Conseil a investi 153 millions de dollars pour mettre de l'art dans la vie des Canadiennes et des Canadiens de tout le pays. Ce livre est financé en partie par le gouvernement du Canada.* We also acknowledge the support of the Ontario Arts Council (OAC), an agency of the Government of Ontario, which last year funded 1,737 individual artists and 1,095 organizations in 223 communities across Ontario for a total of $52.1 million, and the contribution of the Government of Ontario through the Ontario Book Publishing Tax Credit and the Ontario Media Development Corporation.

Canada Council
for the Arts
Conseil des Arts
du Canada

Canadä

Ontario
Ontario Media Development
Corporation

ONTARIO ARTS COUNCIL
CONSEIL DES ARTS DE L'ONTARIO
an Ontario government agency
un organisme du gouvernement de l'Ontario

FSC
www.fsc.org
RECYCLED
Paper made from
recycled material
FSC® C103567

Printed and bound in Canada by Marquis   5 4 3 2 1

For Snaige and Jack
(You made me do it.)

CONTENTS

HERMES REPAID

To prevent me from reading all day long my mother bought a piano.

A piano demonstrated that she had finally got back something of what had been lost by the war. A piano represented culture and achievement, and her youngest son was to be the embodiment of the return to grace. All the better that no one else on our working class street in Weston owned a piano.

Although I had no musical talent, I could use the piano as a form of retaliation upon my much older brothers.

I loved nothing on television so much as movies, especially the old ones and even the corny serials that had once been shown in cinemas before the war. Sunday afternoons were zones of freedom for all of us after church and before finally buckling down to do homework on Sunday nights. Serials and double-header movies played on TV in the afternoon but, sadly, so did *Wide World of Sports*.

My older, more powerful brothers would watch any sport at any time. I didn't begrudge them the baseball and football games on TV, and we all loved hockey, but they would watch anything, from water skiing to pole vaulting to motorcycle racing. I found it a crime that arcane sports, barely sports, trumped my movies. So I sought revenge.

"Why are you playing the piano?"

"I'm practising."

"Why do you have to practise while we're watching TV?"

"I have to practise whenever I can."

"We can't hear the announcer."

To add pungency to my aggression, I played badly, repeating errors without ever correcting them. Playing badly took no extra effort. I did it naturally, to the acute pain of not only my brothers, but also my piano teacher, Mr. Rose.

After giving up on personally teaching me, Mr. Rose kept assigning me to new and different piano teachers in his school. One died, to be replaced by another who liked to mimic students' playing by simultaneously playing on their forearms. After some alert parents had him fired, my next teacher was Frank, a hairy-fingered Italian who taught to make a few extra dollars to supplement his job playing for burlesques at the Blue Angel. Frank had seen it all, and the Tony Bennett knock-off let me bang away unchastised through clouds of his cigarette smoke. If I aggravated his hangover too much, he'd tell me to run across the street to Inch's Drugstore to get him a cup of coffee.

My brothers used the same tactic. "At least bring us some Kool-Aid."

"Why should I?"

"We'll give you a quarter."

"When?"

"As soon as we have one."

I knew their weaknesses and they knew mine. A quarter

would pay for a comic, a bottle of pop, and a small bag of chips. I brought them their Kool-Aids and lived in the dream of collecting the quarters, which were really nothing more than notional coins, bitcoins of the past, because they existed only as abstractions.

Older brothers were mixed blessings. They were frenemies *avant le mot*: champions, teachers, exploiters, torturers, benefactors, and the only ones who really understood you.

Andy and Joe were ten and six years older than me. Andy was practically an uncle, the one who dressed me in the morning when I was still too small to get my own socks on. They were strong, sporting boys. Joe was the only boy in the history of St. John the Evangelist elementary school who could knock a baseball right out of the playground. The two of them could play "goalies" on the driveway for hours with two hockey sticks and a tennis ball. They knocked a lightweight golf ball around nine holes in our suburban backyard and threw footballs out on the street with deadly accuracy.

Naturally, they expected to train me in their skills, but by a cruel roll of the genetic dice, I had come out timorous and inept, the third brother in fairy tales but without the happy ending. Their attempts at coaching could be hazardous.

"Don't be afraid of the ball," said Andy.

"Don't be afraid of the bat," said Joe.

I was backcatcher to my brothers, who were pitching and batting, and I stood well back of the bat, so far back that the ball was already arcing low, making it hard for me to catch.

I wanted to please them, so I did what I was told and pulled up close behind Joe. His bat caught me straight across the forehead on the back swing.

It could have been worse. I could have been hit on the forward swing.

⊗

"Stand over there," said Andy. They had learned a little of my incompetence, and if they couldn't train me, at least they could keep me out of the way. I stood by the back door as the two finished preparations over by the garage. They had devised bolos by putting two hardballs into a pair of complicated string bags and then running a thin rope between them. Bolos were used to wrap around the feet of runaway cattle. We didn't have any cattle. Still, we might have cattle one day, and if we did and the cows ran off, we would have bolos to stop them in their retreat.

Andy swung the one ball around over his head while holding on to the second, and when he finally had enough momentum, he let go.

His aim must have been off.

I had never been hit by two baseballs in quick succession.

My footballs wobbled and never flew very far. Nor could I ever get the hang of catching one of them. I held my hands up, but the ball always flew between them. I was more goalposts than receiver.

Seeking to emulate my brothers, I played on the elementary school hockey team, and I was the only kid in grade four who was often asked not to bother to dress for the game. My enraged immigrant father would shout down at the coach from the stands, but the coach was indifferent. As for me, I was relieved. All skates seemed designed to hurt my ankles.

In my four-year career on the ice, I scored only one goal, and it was disallowed by the referee, based on no rule I had ever heard of, unless it was to grant a career shutout to a hockey player who was not even a goalie.

This difference in temperament extended to other parts of our family life. Andy and Joe ate hamburgers, potato pancakes, and roast pork with gusto. I preferred sautéed mushrooms and could only eat eggs if they were scrambled dry and served on lightly toasted bread that was quartered diagonally.

It drove them crazy to watch my mother prepare special meals for me, the baby who came into the family when my parents had finally reached middle-classdom after years as struggling immigrants. My brothers still remembered the bleak DP camp in Germany and the dreary farm outside Fort William in their early years in Canada.

They had helped my father build our house. At first, they all lived underground in the basement while the place was slowly banged together above them, scattering sawdust on them daily. As for me, I grew up in the completed house in my own bedroom with cowboy curtains and an electric train set. On warm days, I could open my window and listen to the real trains that passed through Weston a half mile away and imagine a better place than the one I inhabited, a place where sports were not the measure of a boy's success.

I escaped into books and became the household reader, occasionally driven outside by my mother, who thought it wasn't healthy for a boy to be inside so much on fine days.

I was no better in sports with boys my age than I was with my older brothers, but the street presented many more options, especially in the empty lots and farm fields that had not been developed yet. There we built catapults and, if we had any money, bought cannon crackers to blow up toy soldiers. War games were played every day, and once my mother called me indoors and gave me two dollars because she was embarrassed that I was using a Luger plastic water gun while the other boys all had long guns. She was mortified to be the mother of the most underarmed kid on the block. We built go-karts whose wooden disk wheels always fell off because we had no axels and used nails instead. We kept up low-level gang warfare with kids on other blocks, using dirt clods as our main weapons. We took child prisoners whose hands we tied up with clothesline, and we held them until they wet their pants or it was time for supper. Indoors, we built telegraph systems using scraps of wire, an old door buzzer, and my electric train transformer. But we never learned Morse code well enough and had to run up and down stairs to confirm the dots and dashes with the sender.

As my brothers and I grew older, the difference in temperaments persisted.

We couldn't really fight because they were so much bigger and stronger than I was, but they had taught me a few tricks. If you can't beat someone with better strength or speed, then beat him any way you can.

I was in grade eight when the friendly janitor, probably bored down in his vast boiler room in the school basement, grudgingly let a few of us boys hang around with him. He was a sincere and effusive Italian and all of us, although on the edge of high school and coolness, still loved boyish things. He opened up the furnace to show us the jet of hot flame that heated the boiler. He let us try on fifty years' worth of costumes from plays and arcane Catholic processions. There were silk capes, tiaras, crowns of thorns, crosses of many sizes and materials as well as dozens of broken plaster saints that he didn't have the heart to throw out. And among these riches, we found a near complete set of boxing gloves.

There were three well-worn twenty-ounce sparring gloves, fuzzy leather pillows. We couldn't find the fourth glove no matter how hard we looked. The janitor was a boxing enthusiast, and he had us try them on and spar. The missing glove was a left, so the boxer who wore only one glove on his right wrapped a towel around his left hand and was permitted to use that hand to block, but not to hit.

Down in that cellar, Vaughn Currigan and John Varneckas and I became enthusiasts, learning to keep our fists up, pulling our punches on the instruction of the janitor. We were all aware that one bloody nose would bring down the wrath of our principal, Mother Cecily. We learned to keep our fists close to our faces, like we'd seen in the movies, and we already knew that hitting below the belt was forbidden.

We boxed before and after school. We learned how hard it was to keep our hands up. And we learned restraint, never going in too hard for a punch.

We took turns taking the gloves home. On my day with the gloves my luck was good because I found my brother Joe there after school before our parents came home. Down into the basement we went, where the Ping-Pong table and the hockey sticks were stored. I was the one with the single glove, and we started to spar.

Joe was bigger and faster than I was, yet I could block most of his punches. But not all. He was being particularly light with me, careful not to hurt me, but he kept making it in with taps on my cheeks and kidneys. He was getting on my nerves and a decade of helpless-little-brotherness was about to be cast off. Joe tended to swing wide. He hadn't been trained by our janitor.

Tap, tap, tap across my cheek and shoulder, and finally I couldn't take it anymore. I thought of the backswing of the baseball bat. I remembered the bolos. The next time I saw an opening, I went in using the forbidden left hand, wrapped only in a tea towel. I went straight to his nose, not too hard but hard enough.

His moment of shock was all I needed. I went tearing upstairs to the ground floor and then up another flight to the bathroom, the only door with a lock on it. He wasn't far behind me, but I had enough of a lead to lock the door and put my foot against the bottom on the inside.

It was like being in a horror movie. He banged on the door and threatened me at the same time that he ordered me to open the door. Any fool knew how to open a bathroom door lock with a bobby pin, but it wouldn't work as long as I held my hand on the inside knob and didn't let the lock mechanism turn.

"My nose is bleeding!" he roared.

But that was a good thing. The closest other sink was in the kitchen, and he eventually had to go down there to get a towel.

I would have to come out eventually, but my parents would come home from work soon and protect me from him. I sat tight and waited.

He couldn't get me then, but we all had long memories. Brotherhood was like the Cold War of the time, mostly uneasy peace with occasional skirmishes. Nuclear war never actually broke out. We saved those conflagrations for exchanges with our father. And at the same time Joe took me under his wing after Andy moved out. We went to James Bond films, and if he couldn't turn me into a good sportsman, at least he turned me into a reasonable fisherman.

We grew older and missed the whole hippie thing because they were too old and I was too young. I felt as if the French Revolution was happening, but I couldn't take part because my parents had grounded me. Worst of all, my mother worked for the Feds as a chemist on street drugs, and she warned me that every police sample came into her building with the name of the accused on it, and it wouldn't do to have the last name we shared on the brown paper envelope.

We may have missed the cultural explosion but we didn't miss the fashions. For a while Joe wore long sideburns and a Fu Manchu moustache, and eventually all three of us had beards. Photographs from this time are painful to look at, decked out as we were in wide ties and long collar points.

Then brotherhood under one roof was over. We all went our own ways. Suddenly, there was nothing to argue about, unless it was politics, and the only sports that ever appeared in our common lives were occasional Super Bowl games we watched together. Even then, I never knew the teams or the players and watched the games as if they were some sort of spectacle, say Kabuki theatre or ballet. But it was better than OK to sit around with them.

They liked to remind me that I was the spoiled one, and I would remind them about how they had beaten me, but these were old stories by the time I turned forty.

There was a big surprise party for me. Such a surprise that I needed two shots of vodka to calm down. Sixty people gathered together from all parts of my past to celebrate the middle of my life.

Near the end of the party, when we were getting ready to go home, my brothers held something out to me.

It was a blue velvet bag with a gold string. I knew it well. Crown Royal whisky used to be sold in those bags. We kids had all loved the bags and put marbles or other treasures in them. They hadn't been made for quite some time.

My brothers didn't say anything and I took the bag. It was kind of heavy. I jerked it up once and heard the clink of coins inside. I looked up at them, uncertain.

"The quarters we owe you. Thanks for the Kool-Aids."

1969

THE ROCKET

The town of Weston was the victim of the City of Toronto, half-consumed but not yet fully digested, still visible like a freshly swallowed frog inside the body of a snake. Not much happened in Weston that would register on the national news, but what happened in the world outside found its muffled way into Weston.

Our high-school principal, in a burst of newfound liberalism, now permitted jeans to be worn to school, and boys with long hair were no longer given the choice between a barbershop and suspension. But the small town atmosphere lingered — old-timers came out to watch the afternoon high school football games; men of all ages wore shiny Weston Dodgers "hockey coats" in fall or winter; any young man with a Saturday-night date would be reasonably expected to spend a few hours in the afternoon cleaning and polishing his father's car, if he could get his hands on it.

My own father believed that a car was like a bottle of liquor: it was a good thing to have, but the more you took from it, the less you would have left. This philosophy never stopped him from drinking quickly, but when it came to the family car, he believed every mile his sons drove would subtract from the total number of miles in its life. Other fathers seemed to think like ours. Father-son battles on driveways were common, especially in the new suburban part of Weston, where everything interesting was too far to walk to and teenagers needed a place to make out.

The sock hop had died and the mosh pit was still waiting to be born. We were stepping hesitantly out of our Archie comic lives; there were still a few Bettys and Veronicas around but the boys they were looking at were Bob Dylan and Frank Zappa.

TV was our window into the world, where the Vietnam War was happening, but so was the moronic comfort of *Gilligan's Island*, a television show so stupid as to achieve camp status. And in 1969, TV was our window to Buzz Aldrin and Neil Armstrong walking on the moon.

In a burst of space enthusiasm my classmate, Les, came to me that September with a book on rockets.

It was the banner year of high school when the homeroom girls were all pretty and the boys were beginning to lose their awkwardness. We had just the right mix in our class of public school kids and Catholic school kids to feel comfortable and thrilled at the same time.

Les was the first guy I knew with a steady girlfriend, red-haired Becky, who came from one of the important local families. Les's mother had divorced and remarried, which wasn't scandalous anymore but still slightly racy and modern. He had brillo-pad hair that would turn into the best Afro I ever saw on a white man a few years later. And he had enthusiasms that he carried around with him like germs — it would take just a little time with him before you were in the drama club, or photography club, or hustling girls outside our Weston hangout, the Central Restaurant. Les loved girls, and even though he had a steady, he considered it his right to flirt. He was amazingly successful at this, and it paid off to be around him because it brought me into the dating game and into my first clash of the sexes.

There were no women involved in our early rocket research. This consisted of studying a handbook on how to build one, with instructions on how to load the chemical engines in a kitchen sink while crouched down so that if the explosives went off, we'd lose nothing more than our hands. My mother was a chemist, but I didn't ask her about explosives because she knew too much. She might try to talk us out of it.

Instead, Les and I walked twenty minutes to the bus stop, rode half an hour to the subway, and then another half hour on the train to get to a hobby shop on Yonge Street. The shop was full of parts for electric trains, balsa wood to make kites and gliders, gasoline-engine model planes that flew in circles off a long wire, and plastic model kits of warships and spitfires.

We asked at the counter for chemicals to make rocket fuel.

"Are you nuts?" The owner was a big, round man with eyeglasses and a cigar.

We showed him our rocket-making book.

"Sure, I know that book. I even know the guy who wrote it. He's got a couple of lawsuits running against him after the explosions. All that material is illegal in Canada."

Everything was illegal in Canada, a country that disappointed us repeatedly when compared to the USA we saw on television. Even Mars Bars and Three Musketeers, chocolates we saw advertised from Buffalo, were not allowed in Canada. We were living in the land of safety and boredom.

"So if we ever made rockets, how would we get them to fly?" asked Les.

"You want rockets, I can give you rockets. Come with me."

He pulled out a broad drawer from underneath the counter. It had four different rocket kits from one to three stages.

"So how do they fly?"

"The kit comes with a chemical engine included, like a big firecracker open at one end. You put a loop of electrical wire into the open part, run the wires back to a switch and a battery, and when you flip the switch, the coil heats up and the rocket takes off."

"How come these are under the counter?" asked Les.

"They're in a legal grey area. The people who banned firecrackers are trying to ban the engines too. So far, they're still legal, but it's better to keep them out of sight."

Les and I looked at one another. We still mourned firecrackers and fondly remembered banned cannon crackers that could blow your finger off if you held on to three of them and set them off in your fist. What we were going to do was almost against the law. The appeal of the rockets was now all the greater.

Our problem was money. We didn't have part-time jobs and my European parents had never heard of allowance and would have scoffed at the idea if they had. Somehow, we scraped together enough money for a single kit with a spare engine, but no launching rod, wires, or batteries. We'd make those or scrounge them somewhere.

"Just take my advice," said the hobby guy, "and don't use a wick to fire the engine. They're almost always too short and you can burn your fingers in the blast."

To do this, we had to do it right. Les would go home and make a launching pad of a thick piece of plywood and a steel rod that stood straight up as a guide to make sure the rocket shot up true. My job was the electrical parts. I owned an electric train, so I had a lot of electrical wire and I had some idea of how to do this. My father had all sorts of odds and ends among his tools, and I found a toggle switch, built a box, and managed to borrow an old car battery that still had some juice in it.

Word got out about what we were doing. Eight boys came with us after school down to the field behind the hockey rink near the Humber River. The car battery was heavy and Les and I took turns carrying it. No one rode bikes in high school then. A bike was good up to grade eight. After that, you left it behind, no matter how far you had to walk. After all, a girl might see you, and a girl would never take a bike-riding boy seriously.

We set ourselves up on the field as officiously as possible. I coiled two thin wires to make a loop and pushed it inside the bottom of the rocket engine as deeply as I could. The launching pad had to lie flat and Les used a small level to make sure it was so. The tips of the rocket fins had to stand perfectly on the pad once the rocket's guide was slipped down over the rod that protruded from the pad. I ran the wires back to my box switch and then the pair of wires that ran from the switch to the battery, and suddenly heard the whoosh and looked up to see I had left the toggle switch in the "on" position.

The rocket had taken off without a countdown.

I craned my neck as much as I could, but the rocket was out of sight. I'd missed the takeoff and I missed the whole flight and I was overcome with bitterness until something tiny blossomed up there in the vast expanse of indifferent blue. The last burst from the engine had fired forward to push out the nose cone and release the parachute, and now the rocket came down elegantly, swinging from its parachute like an angel swinging on a star.

There was a slight breeze and the rocket drifted toward the river. We ran after it, ready to wade into the smelly shallows if we had to save the cardboard tube from getting wet. But we were lucky, and it drifted just short of the water and Les caught it in his hand in triumph. The boys with us were all about the same age: we were in transition; some were shaving like men and some looked as if they belonged in shorts. But what bound us all was the wonder of the thing.

We had to do it again:

This time, I made sure the toggle switch was off before I attached the battery, and this time we had a proper count-down. The engine blast blew out the wires and the rocket shot upward with incredible speed. I watched it until it disappeared, and then waited for the blossom that I knew would come.

We were heroes among all the boys in school the next day, but the girls remained indifferent. Most of them looked like women. We were interested enough in them to wonder at their coolness, to wish they'd admire us even a little, but our enthusiasm stayed boyish to most of them.

Les and I conferred during lunch in the cafeteria, over French fries and gravy and Swiss steak. We got a lot of advice, some of it from boys who had not even been at the launch. Les was nothing if not ambitious. If a single-stage rocket was good, a three-stage rocket would be better.

Since a single-stage rocket shot out of sight, a cooler head might have asked why we needed a three-stage rocket, but there were no cooler heads among us. The important thing now was to get the money. It was useless to ask my father for money. He hated to spend it at the best of times, and spending it on toys was pure foolishness to him. My mother was more sympathetic, but I would need ten dollars for my share, and that was half the cost of a week's groceries. It was too much. I returned empty pop bottles, but we never had many of those and the returns didn't add up to much. I borrowed from my older brothers, but that only brought in two more dollars. My uncle's visit from Detroit brought me up to nine, and Les was too restless to wait any longer, so he put up the last dollar.

But as we were raising money, we were also contemplating a grand enlargement of our project. True men pushed the boundaries. The Americans had put a man on the moon. Twelve years earlier, the Russians had put a dog in space. We wanted to do something equally grand, but our resources were limited. We settled on the idea of sending a mouse into the sky.

They sold them down at the pet shop, where kids bought them as pets and, it was rumoured, keepers of exotic snakes bought them to feed to their animals. At sixty cents for one white mouse, the cost was manageable. Les had to spring for it but he didn't mind. It had been my idea. Now I had an engineering problem to solve, because we could not just put the mouse in the tube of the rocket. The mouse needed its own compartment. Down at my father's tool bench, I determined that the body of the rocket was wider than the tube from a roll of aluminum foil. The one would fit inside the other. I designed the two-inch tube carefully, with air holes on the side, a double cardboard base to protect the mouse from the last upward blast of the engine that would kick out the nose cone and parachute, and finally a sturdy string so the mouse compartment would be firmly attached to the rocket after it was ejected and swung back to earth.

This project seemed noble to us. We were not exactly doing research because we were not discovering if animals could go into space. The scientists already knew that. But we were echoing the achievements of our time. We had not even learned the word yet, but if we had, we would have said we were joining the zeitgeist.

The girls in the class did not share our enthusiasm. Word of the mouse got out, and at first we couldn't even understand what had made them pay attention, unless it was that they had come to their senses about the higher calling we were following. But Elaine and Linda cornered me at the locker alcove. Elaine was sophisticated for our grade. She knew of *Time* magazine and federal politics. She wore glasses and had short, blonde hair, which made her look serious, but she wore a tight mohair sweater that made me want to look at the rest of her. Linda was very quiet — the class brain, the rougher boys called her. She had straight blonde hair and a slim body like something out of the twenties. She was long and lean and smart and I'd danced with her a few times at class parties. Elaine came up close to me, and Linda hung back, but Linda was the one I'd hoped to stand closer.

"Is it true," Elaine asked, "that you and Les are going to send a mouse up in a rocket?"

"That's right. Isn't it incredible?"

"Incredibly stupid and cruel."

I looked at her, not understanding. "Why is it cruel?"

"Because you're going to torture the mouse."

"Nothing is going to happen to the mouse. People have been to the moon. Haven't you been watching TV? A dog went into orbit twelve years ago."

"The dog's name was Laika, and it died."

"Science has come a long way since then."

"Don't be ridiculous."

"Why aren't you talking to Les about this?"

"Because Les is an asshole. I was holding out some hope that you might be a nice boy."

I bristled. To be called a boy by a girl was demeaning, and to be called a nice boy was tantamount to an insult. But what could she have called me? A man? That would have sounded odd. I was somewhere between: just a guy, not yet a man, and most certainly not a boy.

"What do you think about all this?" I asked Linda.

She shrugged. "I think she's right." Linda looked at me with doleful eyes as if I were someone she loved who was doing the wrong thing, the way my mother might look at my father if she found an empty mickey of Five Star Whisky in among the Ajax and Mr. Clean bottles. Of course, my mother would give that look for a moment and then launch into a furious tirade. But Linda didn't do that. She just looked at me.

"I'll tell you this," said Elaine, holding a finger up like someone twenty years her senior, "nothing had better happen to that mouse."

⊠

There must have been fifty of us at the field on the day of the launch. The girls were there too, but the pack of them, six or seven, stayed up on the hill above the field. Not so far away that they couldn't see what we were doing, but not so close as to be complicit. I studied the group and saw that Linda was among them. What was it about her that I found so attractive? There was more to her than met the eye. She was very smart, but too smart to let it show. I thought maybe I loved her at a distance, but wasn't sure how to close the gap.

I'd told Les what Elaine had said.

"Don't worry. She's mad at me, not at you."

"What for?"

"I made out with her for a while at the last party. Then I made out with someone else."

"You mean it's not about the mouse?"

He looked at me like I was a child, and I didn't want to pursue it.

I had brought the mouse in a big mason jar with holes punched in the top because it had eaten through the cardboard box I'd bought it in. It was a pretty mouse, white, with long whiskers and a pink nose. It was accustomed to being handled and did not try to escape from my hand or bite me. I held it in my fist with its small snout sticking out the end, but it was a tight fit to get it into the compartment I'd made for it. The mouse managed to turn a bit and stick its nose out of one of the breathing holes before I slipped the compartment into the rocket and put the nose cone on top. I passed the rocket to Les, and he ran a preflight examination. Did the mouse squeak? If it did, we didn't hear it.

We made everyone stand back. Even the girls came closer,

down toward the base of the slope they had been standing on. Les did the countdown, and I flipped the toggle switch. We had liftoff.

It might have been a good idea for us to study aerodynamics a little more. The designers of the rocket kit had known what they were doing and they had never expected anyone to add a payload. The rocket went high in its first stage, but not as high as the single-stage rocket had gone, and then there was a sort of pause as the first stage blew off. In that moment of no upward thrust, the rocket's nose, made heavy by the addition of the mouse, turned down and aimed at the earth. We scattered. The second stage drove the rocket back toward us with great force and it struck the ground and stuck into it, which was lucky for us. Because if the rocket had been merely lying on the ground, the third stage would have driven it across the field, maybe into the feet of one of the boys with us. But as it was, the third stage simply burned fiercely for a moment, and then the final burst upward made the nose cone eject or, more precisely, made the top of the rocket detach from the nose cone stuck in the earth. And when it did so, it threw out the unopened parachute and the compartment that contained the mouse.

We were frozen for a moment. The girls came down the hill like furies led by Elaine. I didn't look forward to facing her, but she went straight for Les, shrieking at the top of her voice as Les crossed his arms and looked at her ironically, a pillar facing nothing stronger than a stiff breeze.

I walked away. Linda had hung back near the rear of the girls' group.

"Hi," I said.

"Hi."

"It didn't turn out so well."

"No."

"Are you going to forgive me?"

She shrugged.

"Can I buy you a Coke?"

"OK."

We walked up over the hill and into downtown Weston to the Central Restaurant. Behind us, the drama continued to unfold. I learned later that Elaine called Les a murderer, but he claimed the mouse wasn't even dead, only wounded. He took the mouse out of its compartment and found it had a bloody nose, but it was unclear if the mouse was dead or alive. Les said it would be cruel to let a wounded mouse suffer, and he took it by the tail and ran down toward the Humber where he intended to smash it between two stones and then throw its body into the river. Elaine went charging after him, and quite some drama apparently played out on the banks of the river before the stunned mouse was freed.

Linda and I talked for a while in the restaurant. We found it easy to talk. We talked a great deal then, and more in all the years that followed in high school. We were sometimes girl-friend and boyfriend, if a little kissing and fondling counted, but even if we were going out with someone else, we always talked.

But back in high school in the weeks that followed, new dramas unfolded and new parties were gone to. One night, Linda and I were on a bed, making out, when another couple landed heavily beside us. It was Elaine and Les. The mouse was forgotten, and we built no more rockets that year, or ever again.

1970

THE BEER BARREL POLKA

My father was puffing on his pipe by the garage when I walked up Langside Avenue and turned into the driveway at number 22. He was skulking, I thought, as he beckoned me over.

"Your mother tells me she found a Bay Street bus transfer in your pants pocket. Been going downtown?"

My father's question sounded innocent enough, but he was crafty, and I had to watch my step. Bay Street was close to Yorkville, and an admission to visiting Yorkville would have been the end of me.

"Yeah. I wanted to go down to the Hercules store to look at some knapsacks."

"Hercules is right on Yonge. Why did you take the Bay bus?"

He always travelled by car, and he had the worst sense of direction of anyone I knew. Yet somehow, the bus routes were clear in his head. He must have looked them up. I had to tread very carefully.

"It was a nice day. I wanted to stay above ground, so I took the Bay bus instead."

My father nodded, but he was still suspicious. How could he have known about Hercules in the first place? He hated downtown. We lived in the suburb of Weston and my father never went anywhere except to the Lithuanian church and work. With one exception. My father and his Polish and Ukrainian buddies once went to an anti-anti-Vietnam-War demonstration *to give the government an idea of what people really think.* There were a surprisingly large number of those demonstrations, considering that we weren't even in the United States. My father and his friends all wore suits and ties that smelled of mothballs and, in the winter, hats with the ear flaps turned down. A dozen or so would stand on the fringe of some anti–Vietnam War rally and call out slogans with a megaphone: "Bomb give us twenty-five years of the peace."

They could never get the language quite right. Although no one paid much attention to these geezers on the fringe of the mainstream, it kept the more radical Eastern European kids from going to any anti-war rally for fear of being seen by one of their parents' friends.

The Summer of Love, 1967, was only three years behind us, and people in Toronto were still wearing tie-dyed T-shirts and granny glasses. Love was in the air, supposedly, but not enough of it had made it across the border from the States as far as I was concerned. Not only was Canada boring, but Eastern European parents had built their own iron curtain to keep the kids imprisoned in old-fashioned attitudes. The TV stations that came across the airwaves from Buffalo were our own Voice of America that underscored the tyranny of our parents.

I had tried hanging around Yorkville Avenue, hoping that some young missionary of free love would take me into her church, but I was too late for old hippie Yorkville, although our immigrant parents still thought of it as the devil's street.

I knew there was a whole new world out there where people were having sex, drinking beer or even wine outside, and reading Marx, Marcuse, and *Lady Chatterley's Lover*. I wanted desperately to be a part of that world, but if there was a door that brought you into it, I had yet to find it. It wasn't on Yorkville Avenue anymore. Maybe I could dig a tunnel.

"Go inside," my father said. "Your mother has something she wants to tell you."

My mother was mixing a cake. She was always mixing a cake. She made poppy seed cakes that left black dots between your teeth for days. You could clean them out with a toothpick, and a day later a new one would rise to the surface between your teeth, a fossil of yesterday's meal. She also made dense yellow pound cakes and upside down apple cinnamon cakes. The characteristic that all these cakes shared was their dryness. The advantage of this was that they could stand on the table indefinitely. They were made to be eaten with coffee, and if ever a war came and there was a coffee shortage, the cakes could sit on the table and wait a few years until the war ended, rationing ended, and coffee became available again. I wanted Betty Crocker, but my mother would never make anything out of a mix and my father wouldn't eat a frosted cake.

When I got in, she gave me the mixing bowl with two cups of sugar and a cup of hard butter fresh out of the fridge. I had to mix it for her as she stood by the kitchen sink and separated egg whites from their yolks. The butter wasn't even cut up into pieces, and the block kept threatening to shoot out of the bowl like a loose hockey puck.

"I'm worried about you," my mother said. She was dressed

in a green pant suit, pretty fancy for a Saturday with no company. To look at her, you'd almost think she was a real Canadian. (Unlike my father, who might as well have had the letter "I" for "Immigrant" stamped on his forehead.) She *looked* modern, she even listened to Herb Alpert, but she still *thought* like all the other immigrant mothers down at the parish hall. After twenty-five years in the country, she had learned about camouflage.

"I called Mrs. Aldona, and she's agreed to take you on even though you don't have any experience."

Uh-oh. They were taking action, all because of that crummy bus transfer in my pocket. One tiny slip, and I was doomed.

"Doing what?" I asked

"Folk dancing. She runs the Lithuanian Sea Scout Folk Dance Ensemble."

It was important not to laugh. Like gods, my parents seemed able to see deeply into my heart and, like gods, their actions were unpredictable. They crushed me for their sport.

"I don't even belong to the Boy Scouts anymore."

"She's willing to overlook that if you rejoin. I've already bought the uniform shirt and a hat."

I looked through the doorway into the dining room, and there on the table lay the shirt in a new cellophane package and the old-fashioned sailor's hat that looked as if it had come straight off the head of a World War I U-boat sailor.

No amount of sighing did any good.

Why didn't I just refuse? It was tough being a good boy. Good boys suffered more than most. I guess I didn't want to upset them. But my own goodness was killing me.

"Hold my cigarette, will you?" Irene patted her forehead with a Kleenex and adjusted the bobby pins that held on the Lithuanian folk dance costume headpiece, a strange starched sash. She also wore a blouse, vest, skirts, aprons, and sashes that added up to around forty pounds of linen and wool. She looked like a cross between an Easter egg and an unshorn sheep. It was a lot to be wearing as we awaited our turn at the Canadian General Electric Employees' Company Picnic, not a picnic at all, but a barbecue held in the courtyard of the decrepit plant over at Lansdowne and Dupont. It was a grimy building with a watchtower, as if the employees were prisoners who needed to be surveilled all the time. And so they were. Who wanted to go to the dirty brick courtyard on a late spring Saturday when they'd already spent the week at the place? Nobody. But the company picnic was obligatory — it showed team spirit, and we were part of the entertainment.

"How do I look?" Irene asked as she reached forward for her cigarette.

"Great."

And I guess she did, if you overlooked the costume. She had long brown hair, an oval face, like something out of a painting, and a strange little smile at the corner of her lips that you only saw if you bothered to look hard. But who was I to make fun of her costume? I can't say that I was at the cutting edge of fashion with my baggy linen pants, Tom Jones shirt, and long sash. At least I didn't have to wear a headpiece.

"I asked you how I looked," Irene said.

"And I told you."

"But you didn't even really look."

"What's to see between the headpiece and weirdly patterned clothes all over your body? You look like a happy peasant."

"That's just my costume."

"Sure, I'm not blaming you."

But I did. Most of those Lithuanian Sea Scout dancers acted as if the sixties had never happened. They were going to study engineering or secretarial science and then move out to the suburbs. I already lived in the suburbs. I wanted to go the other way.

I feared contamination if I stuck around too much with them. As it was, Mrs. Aldona had me practising waltz and polka steps in my parents' rec room for weeks to get me up to the level of the rest of the ensemble. She was tough. When she told me to practise polka and waltz steps at home for half an hour a night, I listened. I tried to keep the door closed, but my mother or father, and sometimes both, would look in while I was practising.

"Look, Mother," my father said, "somebody finally taught the boy the meaning of fun."

More likely the meaning of fear. The only person I feared more than my father was Mrs. Aldona. She had high blonde hair in ringlets so firm they were unbothered by gale force winds. She was a graduate of the school of withering stares. She majored in irony and sarcasm, with a minor in dramatically hurt feelings, and we always knew she could call our parents at the drop of a hat. Our parents, twenty-five years in-country but still immigrants at heart. To them, even sunglasses were seditious. Who knew what pupils were dilated behind the darkened glass?

Now Mrs. Aldona came around to give us a pep talk just before we went on at the picnic.

"Listen up," she said after she had us formed into a half circle. "We're going onstage after the Ukrainians." Mrs. Aldona paused after the word "Ukrainians" to let its meaning sink in. She paced a bit with her hands behind her back. "The Ukrainians are a tough act to follow. Maybe the toughest. With all that fancy boot slapping and Cossack foot kicking, the crowds love them and, on the surface, it's easy to see why. But all they have is spectacle. You understand? The Ukrainians are no better than Las Vegas. Our dances are quiet, sure, but we have dignity and serenity. People sense that. They respect that. But you have to know how to *project* dignity. Irene, if I ever see you smoking in costume again, you'll get a one-month suspension and a call to your parents. Now go out there and project dignity and serenity or I'll have you practising all summer long."

It was getting late in the program. Kids were crying and some of the older members of the audience were on the verge of heat stroke, but we danced up a storm like moronic peasants at harvest time on the great European plain. I had to admit that one of the advantages of folk dancing was that I got to hold girls a lot. Irene was my regular partner, and I could put my hands pretty much all over her. She didn't seem to mind. For a repressed teenager without a girlfriend, I got all the handholding and waist hugging I wanted.

※

I tried to get to Yonge Street whenever I could. There was a grittiness down there so different from the cleanliness of my home suburb. People still walked around with reindeer sweaters in Weston, and they spent Saturdays washing their cars. The whole day. But on Yonge Street I could almost feel the cosmopolitanism. Girls walked barefoot down the length of the street, all the way down to the pedestrian mall by Simpsons and Eaton's, and pretty young women sold roses out of baskets. If ever I went to San Francisco, I'd know where to get some flowers for my hair. And everybody down there was planning to go to San Francisco sooner or later.

I was standing in the lineup at Zumburger. It was taking forever. The girl in front of me was arguing with the cashier. She turned to me. "What do you think is a fair price for a meat-free bun and fries?"

"With tomato and pickles on the bun," the cashier said.

"You say the condiments are free," the girl protested to the cashier.

"Only if you buy a burger."

"That's not written down anywhere. Let me see the manager."

"He's not here."

"Where is he?"

"Out to lunch."

"You see, even the manager doesn't eat here."

The arguing girl had long, straight blonde hair, like Mary of Peter, Paul, and Mary, and she wore granny glasses and a pea jacket with yellow felt stars and crescent moons sewn onto it.

"Give me two hamburgers, one without a bun," I said. "Give this girl my bun and all the condiments she wants."

The girl in the pea jacket studied me for a while. "I admire what you did."

"It was nothing."

"No, really. People get into fights all the time. We've got to find a better way. Can I join you for lunch?"

Could she?

Joanne was the first vegetarian I'd ever met. She ate tomato and pickle in her hamburger bun, and fries with gravy.

"Gravy?" I asked.

"I'm still in transition. Besides, there's probably no meat in there anyway; just brown."

"Brown?"

"Yeah. It's called brown gravy, isn't it?"

Joanne had already finished high school in Kentucky, where she came from. I'd never met anyone from Kentucky and was surprised that she didn't seem to have much of an accent. Joanne wanted to study in the school of life for a while so she came up to Toronto, where her brother was living as a draft dodger and studying philosophy. She wore her pea jacket even in the summer, and she didn't sweat at all.

"So, how do you like Toronto so far?" I asked.

"It's really clean, you know, but it's a bit off the beaten path up here. I figure my brother's living in exile."

"I know how he feels."

"Were you born somewhere else?"

"No."

She worked on that for a minute. I didn't know what else to say.

After a while, she smiled at me, patted my arm, and kissed me on the cheek. "You're deep. What do you do?"

No one had ever asked me that before, and I thrilled to the question. But what could I answer? It would make me look young to say I was still in school.

"I'm a dancer."

"Neat! What kind?"

"I haven't been at it for very long. I'm still feeling my way along."

"But in general, which way do you lean, classical or jazz?"

"I'm basically into classical right now, but I'm thinking of getting into jazz this fall."

"Stand up. Let me take a look at you."

The only other time anyone had looked at me carefully was when I was a kid being chosen for street hockey. Then, the captains had looked me up and looked me down and passed me over.

"You have very graceful lines," she said. "Like a gazelle."

Someone in the restaurant snorted. What did I care?

Joanne wouldn't give me her number. She said we'd meet again if it was meant to happen. But she'd do an I Ching that night to check.

⊠

Mrs. Aldona worked us like raw recruits that night in the church basement rehearsal hall. We did waltz, polka, and two-step one after the other in quick succession and then collapsed onto the floor for her closing words. Irene was so exhausted, she lay on her back and put her head in my lap. I stroked her hair for a while.

"Next week you dance at Centre Island for Dominion Day. We're going to be up against the Ukrainians again, head to head, and I want you to knock those boot-slappers right out of the competition."

The CHIN multicultural radio station put on a big festival at Centre Island every year. All the local politicos showed up to garner the ethnic vote. All the local ethnics showed up to make sure the multicult funds didn't stop flowing. It was one big festival of interracial, multicultural understanding. And we were going to try to knock off the Ukrainians.

"I wonder why Canadians don't have folk dancing," I said to Irene when Mrs. Aldona was done haranguing us.

"They do. It's called ballet."

I was rubbing my ankle because I'd twisted it a bit.

"I could kiss that spot and make it better," said Irene.

"You're weird."

※

The ferry over to the island was packed, and Irene and I clung to a spot by the railing where we could catch the cool breeze. The city had turned into an inferno. Around us were Italian families with baskets and barely disguised bottles of homemade wine, a few Sikhs in their turbans and a couple of women in saris, Portuguese kids in baseball caps, and a whole contingent of the older immigrants who had never assimilated very well — Hungarians, Poles with their chessboards, Ukrainians, half a dozen other nationalities whose countries couldn't be found on the map. All us immigrants still on the boat after all these years. Even the children of immigrants stayed immigrants. It was like we'd been inoculated against mainstream culture. I wouldn't have been surprised if our ferry travelled down the St. Lawrence and out to the Atlantic and landed at Ellis Island.

Irene was smoking cigarettes and eating the scene up with her eyes, but all I thought about was how we were stuck in the city during the July First weekend. I bummed a smoke from her. Anybody with a car and the money for a tank of gas was sure to be up at Lake Simcoe or Wasaga Beach. The ones with real money were up in Muskoka. As for us, we were still on the boat. Even when we got off the boat, the island was filled with other people like us. Happy ethnics, celebrating their heritage while building a better future together. Other people went to Woodstock. Some had been to Monterey. I was on Centre Island. We had no psychedelic drugs or rock and roll. We didn't have to fear biker gangs. The only good part was the peasant-like unruliness. Whole families were already drinking wine on the grass, and there weren't enough cops to ticket them all, even if they had tried. For one day, we were allowed to drink in public. It was one of the only benefits. I wished I'd thought to sneak over a bottle of my own.

Irene linked arms with me as we walked along the path toward the stage about half a mile off. I didn't pull away.

"I want to ask you a favour," she said.

"Shoot."

"There's going to be a contest later on today, and I want you to enter it with me."

"What kind of contest?"

"A polka contest."

"Come on."

"No, really. It'll be a lot of fun."

"I'm only dancing in this group under protest," I said.

"I see. You're a *rebel* Lithuanian folk dancer, right?"

"There's no way I'm going to join a polka contest."

"But you're good at it. And besides, the prizes are great."

"Like what?"

"Third prize is dinner for two at The Ports of Call."

That didn't sound so bad.

"Second prize is a dozen pairs of shoes each."

"I'd rather get third prize."

"First prize is a colour TV set."

"Each?"

"I didn't ask. I guess so. Even if it isn't, we could sell it and split the money."

My parents wouldn't let me work until I was eighteen. I never had enough money of my own. It didn't sound so bad.

We went out to the bandstand where some of the Ukrainians were already warming up. Our accordion player, Al, was already there, and he strapped on the box and played for a while as Irene taught me a couple of polka variations that might wow the judges, like dancing backwards or turning Irene again and again under my raised arm. She was making me laugh. I needed to stop because I was laughing so hard. Irene didn't look half-bad, really, if I ignored the stupid folk dance costume.

"Did you bring a bathing suit?" I asked her.

"I didn't think of it. Why?"

"Just a thought."

Mrs. Aldona finally showed up, and she made us stop so we wouldn't wear ourselves out for the big showdown with the Ukrainians. We even tried to seem friendly to them, all in the multicultural spirit of things. The Ukrainians invited us to their picnic before the show. They served some kind of kebab.

"This is pretty good," I said to a guy in a Cossack hat. "What's it called?"

"Meat on a stick."

"What kind of meat?"

"I don't know."

"How do I know it's not horse meat or something?"

"Are you making fun of our food? You come as a guest and insult our food?"

"What insult? I was just asking."

"I suppose yours is better. What's your national food?"

"Zeppelins."

"The hot air balloons?"

"Not exactly. It's a football-shaped potato dumpling with meat inside and gravy on top."

"What kind of gravy?"

"Onions, bacon, butter, and sour cream."

He laughed, but I didn't get the joke.

Mrs. Aldona was edgy by the time we had to go on. A lot seemed to be riding on this performance. By now, it was hotter than it had been at the General Electric plant and some of the picnickers were boozed up after drinking wine all morning. The Eastern Europeans had been sucking on mickeys. We got a few catcalls from the drunks when we started to dance but, let's face it, who can out-shout an accordion? We danced OK, nothing special, but we still won the trophy because one of the ferries had a mechanical failure and half a dozen Cossacks were left drifting around Toronto Harbour for the afternoon. Irene was in a hurry to get us over to the polka contest, but Mrs. Aldona held us all up. Her eyes were gleaming. Clearly, she was in some kind of folk dance teacher heaven.

"Kids," she said, "I have some news. I didn't want to hint at this until I got confirmation of funding, but there was a federal government envoy in the crowd. We've been in touch. The Canadian government is moving into major funding of our endeavours, and with their help, we'll have enough money to tour Europe next summer. Just think, kids, we're going to dance in London, Paris, Milan, Innsbruck, and Stuttgart. It's a world tour!"

Mrs. Aldona was pretty excited, and she talked for so long that Irene and I didn't have a chance to get changed back into our civvies. If we were going to make the polka contest at all, we would have to go as we were. I had to carry Irene's bags for her because she needed to hold up her skirts as we whipped across the island. Our costumes didn't raise an eyebrow. There were kimonos, kilts, and bear hats all over the place. What was a pair of gaily dressed Eastern Europeans?

We made it just in time to register and get numbered, and then we went into a roped-off circle in the grass where an accordionist struck up the "Beer Barrel Polka" without the least bit of warm-up. We danced for around ten minutes. Then an announcer started to explain about the contest over the tops of our heads, but we were supposed to keep on dancing.

It wasn't all that easy to dance on grass, and with all the rushing around, our own stage performance, and the practice we'd had that morning, I was bushed within a few minutes and sweating right through my costume.

"Just keep dancing," Irene said through a gritted-teeth smile. She could read me pretty well. We'd been dance partners for months by that time.

It was a hot day in a hot summer, and I thought I might faint, but we were doing OK. There were only about another thirty couples. When I thought I'd gone past my limit and then found some second wind, the judges started coming out into the crowd and eliminating couples by tapping on their shoulders. Miraculously, we made it past two rounds of cuts, and the judges announced a five-minute break before the last ten couples took it down to the wire. I was set to collapse, but Irene made me stay upright and drink my glass of water daintily, just in case the judges were watching.

"The trick to these things is to make it all seem easy," said Irene. "Sweat visibly, or look strained, and everyone knows you're a loser."

"So how am I supposed to sweat invisibly? I'm soaked right through."

"Ignore it. Think of Queen Elizabeth. You do what you have to do. That's what made Anglo-Saxons the rulers of the world."

"Jesus, Irene, you must be suffering from dehydration or something. I can barely understand you."

There was no time for her to explain because the music started up again. That same polka, that same damn polka, over and over again. Accordions, beer barrels, and folk dancing. I could barely stand it. But for all my disgust, we seemed to be doing well. The judges kept walking out and tapping other couples on the shoulder until there were only four of us left on the circle of grass. If we could keep it up, there was a chance we'd be in the money.

Joanne was standing in the front row, still dressed in her pea jacket. I didn't know if she'd been there from the first or if she'd just arrived. It didn't matter. She was looking straight at me with a look as severe as Mrs. Aldona's at her worst. Around and around I turned, with Irene in my arms, but on every circle

I looked at Joanne, and her severity did not soften.

I had the sense, then, that I was awfully close to something. There was a danger I would lose it unless I acted dramatically. I could dance the "Beer Barrel Polka" for the rest of my life, or I could go for Joanne. The choice was obvious. I let go of Irene and she stumbled back a little with the unexpected momentum.

"Hey," Irene said, far more quietly than I would have done if my partner had done the same to me. The judge was already out on the circle to tap the next couple on the shoulder. Maybe it didn't matter that I'd just ditched Irene and thrown my ten pairs of shoes to the wind. I didn't care. I wanted Joanne.

But Joanne saw me coming and she took off. She was incredibly fast, the girl from Kentucky in the pea jacket. I chased her for a few hundred yards but there wasn't much hope. She drew farther and farther away. Once her lead was insurmountable and I had stopped to gasp for breath, she stopped too, far ahead of me, and waved me away. I was desperately short of air. There wasn't enough of it on the whole island.

※

The ferries landed in a couple of spots, and I waited for Joanne around Ward's Island, off the beaten track, thinking that would be where she'd go to escape from me. I waited patiently at the dock, watching for her through the crowds that left every half hour and then later, in the evening, every hour. I didn't see Joanne, but Irene showed up at the second-last ferry at eleven. She was dressed in civvies and she had my clothes in a bag as well. I was leaning up against the railing by the ferry, looking out at the bright lights of Toronto's skyscrapers as they loomed over the island.

"Did you catch her?" Irene asked.

I shook my head. Irene didn't say anything for a while.

"I'm waiting," she finally said.

"What for?"

"Your apology."

I just looked across the water to the skyscrapers of Toronto. They looked pretty good. When Irene saw I wasn't going to say anything, she did.

"I had my heart set on winning that prize. So I thought I'd set up a little prize system of my own, as a sign of my appreciation. If you'd taken us into the winner's circle, I'd have given you a little something. Are you getting my meaning? I wouldn't have promised you any more than first base, but who knows what you'd have been able to steal once you were in the running?"

She walked onto the ferry, and I didn't have the heart to follow her.

※

That pretty much wrapped up the Lithuanian Sea Scout Folk Dance Ensemble season for that year. We were going to start up again in late October, but I wasn't really looking forward to running into Irene again. Over the summer, I'd heard she started dating our accordionist. I don't know what she saw in him. I dated a couple of girls once or twice, but nothing really worked out.

It didn't turn out to be the last time I saw Joanne. I ran into her at a football game at Leaside Collegiate. I'm sure it was her, although she denied it when I spoke to her in the stands. She had the same granny glasses and the same pea jacket, but she claimed she'd never seen me in her life, and it threw me into confusion. Her friends pointed out that she didn't have an accent. Anyone from Kentucky would have been sure to sound different.

1971–1974

SUMMER LESSONS

"You want to go away to another city to study in university? And you think we're going to pay for it?" my father asked. "The answer is no. Don't even think about it. Go to school here in town, pay your own tuition, and consider yourself lucky that we'll feed you and clothe you. And by the way, learn to work with your hands. It'll teach you that you probably won't like doing that. And one more thing. Learn some values from the people you work with instead of daydreaming all the time."

※

The factory made everything from window cleaner to paint stripper. All of us who worked there waded through a stew toxic enough to bring on the apocalypse. And we did it with only one complaint. We were not permitted to smoke on the factory floor.

I worked in liquids, among three giant stainless steel blenders, and then I sloshed around in a few inches of overflow until it ran out through the holes in the floor. Where it went after that was a mystery, but I sometimes caught familiar chemical smells when I was walking along the banks of the Humber River.

42

I thought nothing then of climbing the homemade wooden ladder up to the swaying platform to stir a giant open vat. The foreman told me to wear a facemask and gloves, which meant I was supposed to be careful. Usually, nobody paid much attention to safety. Excessive attention to safety was for wusses. I climbed up to the open vat and pulled up the long metal pole that was my stir stick. I had no instructions on how long to stir, so I did it for about five minutes and then climbed back down.

"What was that stuff?" I asked the foreman when I saw him later on.

"Sulphuric acid." He laughed. "If you'd fallen in there, we could have drained what was left of you through the bunghole at the bottom."

Somewhere in the air there was the idea that work ennobled us. Maybe it had drifted across the world from the Cultural Revolution.

The men were authentic. They were real. But they had habits that did not necessarily seem worth emulating. They banked with the lunch truck driver who came around at noon. The workingmen ate lunch all week on credit and then cashed their paycheques with him on Fridays when he would deduct the costs of the week's fried egg sandwiches and jelly doughnuts. By Monday, they were broke again.

Life lessons happened in the wood-panelled lunchroom. I thought I had it bad working in the perpetual ooze of the wet room, but all the men who worked in the powder rooms had it worse. They came in with gauze facemasks hanging under their chins and sores all over their faces where the caustic soda had blended with their sweat and taken off layers of skin.

Mike, the powder room foreman, commanded not only his team but the whole lunchroom. He used his charisma to enlighten us. He was neat and tidy, like a gas station attendant in the fifties, and he had worked at the firm for ten years. He was steady; he had built his own house by hand out in the country where he and his stay-at-home wife were raising two daughters. He was also a hunter who professed deep love for nature. Good work ethic, good hygiene, strong manual skills, and an attachment to family. Who could be a better model?

"My daughter brought home a stray cat," he said one day when we were drinking the weak coffee and eating the arrowroot biscuits the company provided. When Mike talked, people listened. "I told her I didn't want any cats in the house because of what they did to birds."

"How did that work out?" I asked.

"Poor dear. The cat brought in a dead bird last Sunday, so I took the cat out in the backyard and shot it."

The room was quiet. Finally, someone asked, "What kind of gun did you use?"

"Shotgun."

"Bit of a mess then, eh?"

"Yep."

"How did your daughter take it?" I asked.

"She'll get used to it. She hasn't talked to me for a week, but she'll come around."

Nobody said anything else. We didn't even look at one another.

※

"Don't you ever worry that the hormones might still be floating around here at night?" I asked.

"You'd know it soon enough," said Gerry. "You'd start to grow breasts, and so far neither one of us has those."

Men were forbidden during the day in certain rooms in the birth control pill factory, but we were allowed in at night when a dozen of us worked as the cleaning crew. I was standing in the janitor's closet with Lieutenant, pronounced the Canadian way and sometimes shortened to Lefty. He was tall and white-haired and stooped and his friend, Gerry, was slight.

We spread out during the vast plant at night, each of us doing floor waxing or desk cleaning, only to meet for lunch in the cafeteria. The place was brightly lit, but spooky in an industrial sort of way, especially down near the animal rooms where I could hear the occasional small noises. I was the new man and worked on toilets, and that meant I passed through the territories of other janitors at various times throughout the night.

The place had rules, mostly unspoken. If you pulled out a smoke, you immediately handed out cigarettes to anyone else who was around. If you were too busy at the moment to smoke the offered cigarette, you still took it and tucked it above your ear for later. There were no nonsmokers among us.

Toward the end of the night, Lefty and Gerry could always be found in the closet in the birth control pill pressing room, waiting to make it down to the changeroom to clock out. I liked the two of them because both were old-school military, and Lefty had spent the entire war in a Japanese prisoner of war camp after the fall of Hong Kong. He didn't talk about it much, but he wore the upbeat yet fatalistic resignation of characters in old war movies. He might be going to his death, but he wouldn't make a big deal about it.

"So what's the biggest risk you ever had in your life?" I asked him, prodding him a bit for a story from his King Rat prisoner of war days.

"My biggest danger came right in this room," he said. "They asked me to clean out the inside of the vaginal foam vat. I forgot to wear my watch and I was still in there when the day shift started and somebody came in and closed the lid."

"What happened?" I asked.

"They got him out," said Gerry, "but he had breasts for a while."

"Just size A cup," said Lefty.

I was making my way back through the empty corridors when Jonathan came around the corner and gave me a start. He was Jamaican and had a thick accent that I found hard to understand sometimes. He had an easygoing manner, which was just as well because the others all ribbed him mercilessly.

"What's wrong with you?" he asked innocently when I leaped back.

"You startled me."

"You shouldn't be so jumpy."

"I can't help it."

"Nothing scares me," said Jonathan.

I was irritated by his equanimity. "I could scare you."

"No, you couldn't. I have a calm temperament or I wouldn't be working in this place."

✖ ·

There were rules for lunch in the birth control pill factory. Most of the men brought TV dinners, and a rotating volunteer would put them all in the oven half an hour before the lunch break started.

After most of us had eaten and were just starting to light up and pour coffee, I asked Jonathan to borrow the key to his janitor's closet because I was out of rags. He was being quizzed about his upcoming marriage that weekend, and he passed me the keys. I went down to his closet, opened the door and lowered a broomstick to keep it open, and then ran back with the keys.

I had to move fast. The others were beginning to butt out their smokes when I made a dash back to Jonathan's closet, took out the broomstick, and pulled the door shut behind me.

I turned off the light and waited in the dark.

When Jonathan opened the door, I grunted like an animal and leaped out in front of him. He blinked a couple of times and smiled.

"Did I scare you?" I asked.

"Not really. I'm getting married this weekend. I have other things on my mind."

✕

When I made it over to Lefty and Gerry's janitorial closet later that night, I found them expecting me.

"We thought you weren't going to show," said Gerry.

"Why not?"

"We need a favour. Did Jonathan invite you to his wedding?"

"Sure. He invited everyone."

Summer Lessons   47

"Are you going?"

"I've never been to a Jamaican wedding. I thought I'd go and check it out."

"Well, we all bought him a gift and we were wondering if you could take it."

"Sure," I said. "I'll take the gift. Why, isn't anyone else going?"

"We're all busy this weekend, and besides it's not our kind of thing."

Jonathan lived out in Scarborough, in the east end of town. I didn't know the area all that well, and when my girlfriend and I arrived late at the house, the ceremony was already underway. It was a big suburban house with a combination dining room/living room and a recreation room downstairs. The minister was addressing the bride and groom upstairs and there were so many people jammed in there that we couldn't get within three people of the door. Instead, my girlfriend and I went downstairs, set the big gift on the table, and stood around talking to a few others who couldn't fit upstairs either. Hot food and liquor were already available, so I made myself a rum and Coke and laid some curried chicken over rice on my plate.

I had never eaten Jamaican food before. I had never drunk overproof rum. The rum burned my mouth, so I ate some chicken. The chicken burned my mouth, so I drank some rum. The circle was unbroken. I cut the drink with Coke for the next half hour and felt as I'd had three drinks instead of one.

We chatted with some of the people downstairs. They were wearing colourful shirts and they were friendly enough but I mostly smiled and nodded because I couldn't follow a lot of the Jamaican accent.

Upstairs, the ceremony was taking a long time. There seemed to be a lot of singing. There may even have been some sort of testifying because the odd person seemed to shout in a happy way. My girlfriend and I stuck around long enough for the ceremony to finish and the crowd to begin to come downstairs. I saw Jonathan across the crowd and waved to him.

My girlfriend and I had two more parties to go to, so we eased ourselves out and moved on. She hadn't had any of the rum. She drove.

"So that was unusual," she said.

"What?" I was in a bit of a rum daze.

"We were the only white people there."

Back at work, the others asked me about the wedding and they laughed when I told them about the hot curry and the overproof rum. Jonathan himself wasn't there because he was off for a week on his honeymoon.

When he came back, he took a lot of ribbing over lunch. The men kept asking him the first thing he had done after going off on his honeymoon. Jonathan laughed and said he had put his new wife "over his legs." We all got the idea, but we'd never heard it put anything quite like that before.

Later that night, I was walking down one of the long, lonesome corridors, carrying a sack of tampons to refill the machines in the women's bathrooms. I had been instructed that if I had to go to the bathroom myself, I should never use the women's bathroom, only the men's. There was a code of sorts, and I was expected to adhere to it even if there were no women in the building at night.

I heard a long, low whistle from down the end of a dark

corridor, and as I walked over there, I saw Jonathan coming out of the shadows.

"Hey, man," he said, "didn't I scare you this time?"

"I guess I'm not scared anymore."

"Let me tell you something. You're the only one here who's not scared. The others, they make jokes, but when it comes to me, they are trembling all the time."

⊠

Bread and miniature cakes were my work, not my pleasure, and they gave me some idea about how prostitutes might feel about sex.

I drove five routes that summer, giving a day off to each of the regular drivers, and each route had its kinks. Doing the Oakville suburban route was easy because the regular bread truck driver had had a heart attack, so they gave him a light load. The neighbourhood was full of retired white people with a certain income. I sold a lot of raisin bread in Oakville.

Yonge Street from the highway down to Eglinton was probably the most intense because the traffic and parking were so bad that I had to stop in front of fire hydrants all the time to service the Chinese-run groceries, and I risked even more around the no-stopping times during rush hour when some keen green hornet might play it by the book and make me lose a whole day's income with the traffic ticket. Wonder Bread was our premium brand, and it went down well in that expensive part of town.

Keele Street was a killer because the route was long, long, long, with vast distances that could slow me down if somebody blew a radiator or had a flat. There were some Jews up in the higher end, so I sold a decent number of Silverstein's rye, with preference for marble with no caraway seeds. But down in the southern end it was mostly Italians who resented the fact their kids wanted toast bread, but they stocked it in their groceries anyway.

Rexdale was suburban too, but working class suburban. There seemed to be a lot of kids in that neighbourhood, because the brownies, butter tarts, lemon tarts, Twinkies, and pound cake slices all flew off the shelves.

I loaded the long van every morning at the massive Christie's plant down on Lakeshore. White or brown, whole wheat or rye, it all had to be loaded on the truck and if I wanted to get a jump on the day, I was loading by five to be on the road by six at the latest. We drivers envied the cookie salesmen, whose products could stay on the shelves for weeks and months. Not bread, though. Bread's life was limited. Put too much on the shelf, and the foremen were unhappy with the stale loaves I brought back a week later. Put too few on the shelves and the storekeepers roared at me for disappointing their customers and making their stores look empty.

I rode high in the single seat, van doors open on both sides and never bothering with the seatbelt. Foreman Steve, who had trained me, taught me to light up cigarettes only at red lights and to parallel park the big van with no more than a couple of inches free on either end. I wore a Christie's shirt, so that was what people called me. All the delivery men called each other by their company names when we were waiting in line to unload at supermarkets.

The Queen Street West run was decrepitly urban, with a few factory lunch bars and corner stores where the only bread that sold was Brookside, the bargain brand. I didn't bother to load the truck with Buttercrust, French Loaf, Wonder Bread, Swiss Stick, or any kind of brown on Queen Street. On that route, the customers wanted the cheapest bread they could get and they weren't putting anything more expensive than marge and baloney on top of it.

It was an ugly street. The fine old Victorian shops were crumbling, with a lot of used appliance stores among them. The diners fed the workmen from the Dickensian factories filled with dust and metal shavings. Snot-faced men and women hung around the mental health centre and the old men who'd immigrated after the war and never moved out to the suburbs sat on benches or played chess, wearing winter coats right into the summer. The old hotels where I delivered hamburger buns smelled of cigarette smoke and stale beer, with ageing bachelors living in the rooms upstairs. A decade later, the artists and musicians would start to move in, but not yet. Queen West was a dying street, waiting to be reborn.

But the lady in Betty's grocery store was not going down without a fight. She had old-fashioned wooden shelves, a few bins of onions and potatoes and apples and oranges, and a refrigerated display case that held Kraft cheese slices, mock chicken loaf, baloney, and ham that she sold by the slice, as well as a couple of cartons each of milk, cream, and orange juice. The floor was worn green linoleum with seams where the sheets met, and the door even had a bell that tinkled so she could come out of her adjoining living room whenever a customer appeared. Betty had dyed black hair and a slight European accent of some kind.

And she hated my bread record book with a passion.

"Hey, Christie," she said, "don't look in the book."

But I had to look in the book. That was how we figured out sales patterns and how many loaves to leave.

"You never sell more than three loaves on a Tuesday," I said, "so if I give you four, you're safe even if you have an unexpected purchase."

"And how do you think that makes my bread shelf look?" she asked. I looked at the wooden shelf. It could have held a dozen loaves in its day, but the glory days of the store and its street were long past. I looked down in the book. She hadn't sold any more than four loaves anytime in the last two months, and we were heading into summer, when bread sales went down as people left town on vacations.

I looked at her. This was a strong woman. No man in the picture as far as I could tell, and if she had any children, they were grown up and gone. She wore a lot of makeup, it was true, and the deep red on her lips looked old-fashioned but she didn't look bad, considering. She was keeping herself together, keeping up appearances.

The doorbell tinkled and a rubby came in. We didn't call people street persons yet and we didn't call them homeless. Old-timers called them hoboes and romantics called them vagabonds. But rubbies were drinkers who got their name by mixing rubbing alcohol with wine, and they came in various degrees of bad shape. The worst stank, but this one wasn't that far gone. He wore a winter coat although I was in short sleeves and he had the standard lined rubby face: yellow skin and unkempt white hair.

Betty looked at him. I was a salesman, and if a customer ever came in, he had priority. That was OK. I waited.

"Do you have money?" Betty asked.

He opened his hand. There were a lot of small coins there and even a couple of crumpled one-dollar bills.

"You're rich," she said. She took his money and carried it over to the counter and counted out some change, picking the smaller coins. The rubby wasn't paying attention. He had his eyes on the shelf behind her. She reached back there for a big bottle of vanilla extract. He went for it, but before he could get it in his hands, she took the rest of the money, stretched over the counter, and put it in his coat pocket.

"Don't forget where it is," she said, and she handed him the bottle.

He hadn't said anything before and he didn't say anything now. He turned and walked out the door, tinkling the bell on the way out.

"You sell him vanilla," I said.

"The wine store doesn't open until noon. What's he supposed to do until then?"

I looked out the window and saw a green hornet coming along. He had a pad open and he was writing out tickets on the illegally parked cars. I hated green hornets and I hated their books.

I closed my bread book. I let Betty have all the loaves she wanted, foreman be damned.

※

It was very hot in the back of the panel van and Jennie finally pulled off her T-shirt, wiped her chest with it, and let the shirt drop at her side. The important thing was not to stare at her. There were eleven of us in the van, Les and his girlfriend up front and nine of us in the back sitting on the folding stage with our tents, clothes, and sleeping bags piled up around us and a small space cleared for the pop can ashtray and the cards in the game of euchre that four of us were playing.

"You'd make more money in the bread truck," my father had said. He was right, but there were no undressed girls in the back of my bread truck.

We were actors, and actors were relaxed about their bodies. A couple of the women were feminists too, and to make a big deal about bare breasts would have been amateurish, gauche, and sexist. Luckily, Jennie was my euchre partner and sitting across from me. I had a moment, a very short moment, when my eyes had to go from my cards to look up at her eyes, and in that microsecond, I managed to glance at her breasts.

We were a travelling troupe that played to children's summer camps, not exactly what the federal government had in mind when it created a summer job program for youths, but we somehow got funded by a hippie Ottawa bureaucrat. We were a concept group, like the Beatles' *Sgt. Pepper's Lonely Hearts Club Band* album, and so we called ourselves *Bananas for Everyone*. We didn't know what it meant, so we spun a new story every time a small town newspaper reporter interviewed us.

I felt good being with these people. I was stepping into the world I longed for at last, something I had viewed only from the television screen so far.

Les, my rocket-builder buddy of grade ten, wore an Afro now, and luckily enough for him, although he was white, his hair was curly enough to make his look plausible. Like the Beatles, Les had undergone a transformation. I wanted to undergo a transformation too.

Les looked in the rear-view mirror. "Put your shirt back on," he said. "We're pulling into the next camp."

We rolled from summer camp to summer camp, putting on our knock-off of *The Little Prince* and giving lessons in stage fighting and costume-making. We were a freebie activity for the summer camps, but not all of them wanted us. Our name was a little suspicious, but back in the winter Jennie had tied back her long hair into a ponytail and worn eyeglasses and a business suit. She met with camp directors back in the spring to set up the schedule. She had carried a briefcase and a clipboard and convinced enough directors to make up a tour that got us the OK from Ottawa.

But Jennie in the van was different from Jennie the saleswoman. Now Jennie put her shirt back on.

There were no windows in the back of the van, so we travelled blind in sweat and cigarette smoke with the occasional breeze blowing back from the windows at the front. Les rolled to a stop and talked to someone at the camp gate. We waited for a while and then the van went on and we could hear gravel under the tires.

"Try to look decent," said Les. He stopped the van and we slid our side door back and stepped out.

Facing us on the gravel was the welcoming committee, half a dozen counsellors in pastel polo shirts and tan trousers and the director in the same uniform, but with the addition of a baseball cap to hide his thinning hair.

"Jennifer, is that you?" he asked when we stepped out to meet them. We were sweaty and unkempt and smelled of cigarette smoke. The guys' hair was too long and two of the girls wore love beads. It turned out we had arrived at a Christian camp. We were Easy Riders, entering alien territory. To the shock of the director, we barbarians were inside the gates. And who had insinuated this Trojan horse into his clean-cut universe? Jennie.

I watched her smooth her hair and step forward. She too, like the camp director, now had a clipboard in her hand and her back stiffened as if she was being called to attention in a military drill.

"I'm sorry if we look a little weathered," she said. "We've been on the road, and as you can see, the only van we could afford is pretty small and we all get a little sticky. But we'll be ship-shape for the show tomorrow afternoon."

The director looked doubtful. Jenny sounded a bit like the young Jennifer he remembered, but the visual message the group behind her was sending did not make him feel confident. As for me, I felt I'd just come under the disapproving eye of one of the nuns who had taught me in elementary school.

"And I guess you have nowhere to stay?"

"Why, Mr. Heathcoat," she said, "you promised us a patch of ground where we could set up our tents."

He nodded ruefully and went into a lengthy explanation to Les about a meadow, across a field and through a wood on the other side of the lake. In other words, as far away from the kids as possible. We packed ourselves back into the van and took the rutted route to a hollow a mile away, a place where the senior counsellors had their own campfires on their days off.

We had everything we needed on our side of the lake. We had water and food and a pair of gallon jugs of wine. We'd been doing our show for three weeks already and we didn't need to rehearse. As for the collapsible stage, we'd put that together the next morning.

Jennie had a boyfriend back in town and I had a girlfriend away in Europe for the summer, but since we were friends and colleagues, she and I slept side by side in my tent along with Les and his girlfriend. Nothing was supposed to happen and, sadly for me, nothing had. But every night her head was a foot away from mine and I could smell her hair and tell if she'd been sitting by the campfire.

Les and Rick gathered firewood and I set up the Coleman stove to make dinner. Most of the actors claimed to be vegetarians, but they would eat whatever I made. Tonight it was spaghetti and breakfast sausages. I bought them because they were small and because they were easy to fry, and I bought a lot because I knew the vegetarians would be eating them once they had some wine. We had principles but we backslid all the time.

Jennie and two of the other girls swam before dinner and when I saw them go in the lake, I took a break from the kitchen and joined them. None of them wore tops. The women who did wear tops did not go swimming because it would have been uncollegial to wear them. There were rifts within the women in our group, some more modest than others. As for the young men, we were all trying to navigate the rules in our evolving tribe.

Rick didn't like to swim, but he stood by the grassy lakeside with me. He was a natural performer, a wisecracker who played to any audience available. He sang a camp song to the topless women:

> Granny's in the cellar
> Lordy can't you smell her
> Cooking biscuits on her dang old dirty stove.
> In her eye there is some matter
> That is dropping in the batter
> And she whistles as the [sniff] runs down her nose.

This got him a couple of smiles, but no other response. "Why are you wearing bottoms?" he asked the women.

"Stupid question," Jennie called from out where she was treading water.

"Why is it a stupid question?"

"We're free. We can swim total dressed or totally undressed or something in between."

We were hippie-influenced suburban kids but in our own eyes we were rebels, questioning the dull and stupid conventions of the world we inhabited. We just weren't sure what our new rules were going to be.

"Besides," said Becky, "how attractive do you think it is to see a string hanging down between your legs?"

"Huh?" asked Rick.

They laughed. They were a bevy of nymphs, powerful goddesses of the water, and their laughter was as painful as a set of arrows, piecing heart, pride, and manhood. Rick shrugged to show his indifference to his wounds and slinked away. I was permitted to paddle around their perimeter.

By the time we had finished dinner and the sun was beginning to set, we heard a distant roar and saw a motorcycle coming along the track.

When the man stepped off his bike and took off his helmet and sunglasses to reveal his long, straight hair, we saw it was Ben, our caseworker from Ottawa.

Everybody was an Easy Rider then, even the pencil pushers in Ottawa. A decade earlier he would have been in a white shirt and tie and checking boxes off a form. But not now. Ottawa was home to radical government employees who thought of other things besides their pensions.

He had come for two reasons. The first was to make sure we were fulfilling our mission as we had written it out and had it confirmed by Ottawa. The second was to bring us a few joints to share over the campfire.

Ben was our boss, a good five or six years older than the rest of us, and we huddled happily with him around our campfire in the hollow as night came on, sipping from our second gallon jug of wine and taking the odd toke as the joint was passed around. When the marijuana kicked in, the last of the vegetarian holdouts went over to the Coleman stove and finished off the breakfast sausages.

We talked and talked and Ben pointed out the irony of our ragtag group of wannabe Woodstockers on the far side of the lake from the Christian kids. They represented one world and we represented another, at least in our minds. For now the two worlds existed together in suspension, but the times, Ben implied, were a-changing.

Each of us reacted differently to the wine and cannabis. Some talked loudly, Becky fell asleep, and I got restless and got up to walk around, coming up from the hollow where we had our fire to the shore of the lake where we had swum earlier that day. I could smell the water and hear the frogs. It was a moonless night and the stars shone all the more brightly for it. Across the lake I could see the glow of the fire the Christian kids were sitting around. I could hear them singing their own song, some kind of hymn.

"Do you know it?"

It was Jennie standing beside me. She took my arm the way a European might, as if we were about to walk together down some boulevard. I was raised a Catholic. I didn't know Protestant hymns.

"It's 'Jerusalem,'" she said. "It's a funny hymn to sing at a campfire. And you know what else?"

I didn't.

"It's an Anglican hymn. Can you hear the words?

> *Bring me my bow of burning gold*
> *Bring me my arrows of desire*
> *Bring me my spear: o clouds unfold*
> *Bring me my chariot of fire*

How could a shirtless actor, the object of my own desire, know an Anglican hymn unless she was, or at least had been, an Anglican too? And there was no irony in her voice. She wasn't mocking the kids the way that Ben did.

"Come on," she said. "Let's go to bed."

My idea of her kept getting upended. She was remote, she was intimate, she was a hippie, she was an Anglican. And now this. I was bewildered, yet hopeful.

The invitation wasn't clear. Sometimes going to bed simply meant going to sleep. And since she wasn't being particularly affectionate as we walked back to our tent, I guessed that was what she meant. We undressed to our T-shirts and underpants. The zipper of my sleeping bag faced the zipper of hers, and I left mine open but heard her zip up her own. I resigned myself. That was OK. She had held my arm for a while back at the lake. At least I could lie close beside her. Her hair smelled of the lake. We turned toward each other.

"I have a boyfriend," she said quietly.

"I know."

"And you have a girlfriend too, don't you?"

"I guess."

She reached out with her hand and gave me a light slap.

"You're terrible, you know. But so am I. I just want to say something to you."

"OK."

"Once this finishes and we have to go back to Toronto, we go back to our own worlds, whatever they might be."

I was staying in town to go back to school. She and her boyfriend, as far as I could remember, were going to hitchhike out west.

Maybe it was the cannabis, or maybe the summer night sky we had been under before we crawled into our tent. But for whatever reason, I said the words.

"There is no time but now."

As soon as the words were out of my mouth, I was afraid she might laugh. But she didn't. Then I waited in the hope that I would hear the sound of the zipper on her sleeping bag coming down.

1976

THE BAREFOOT BINGO CALLER

"Shake them balls," somebody shouted out through the silence, and the crowd laughed as it always did the first time it heard that command each night.

Six hundred men and women sat at banquet tables on the floor in front of my stage, and another two hundred were up on the balcony. Seven hundred and fifty of them were smoking. The pitiful nonsmokers lit candles on the tables in front of them on the theory that the heat drove away the smoke from their eyes. The flames were faint stars in the smog.

The audience was industrious, like a foreman's dream of a highly productive factory, each of the men and women focused on laying down the tiny plastic disks on the cards in front of them. The real pros, the hardcore, could handle a dozen cards at a time, but most played six or eight, cigarettes in their left hands and a horizontal column of disks in their right hands, laid out with fast thumb moves. The ushers roved silently among them, extra cards and cash in their carpenter's aprons.

As for me, I had the mike up to my mouth as I sat in the caller's chair and Ping-Pong balls flew up on an airstream and then shot randomly into a slot. I plucked the most recent ball and read out the letter and number on it. The other balls were

63

visible in the Plexiglas box, dancing on the airstream. There was no way to shake them.

Bruno, the manager with his gold tiepin and stiff, wavy hair, was watching me from the balcony. I was under suspicion. I'd been riding the crowd hard, rushing the evening. The only thing I could do was vary the speed at which I called the numbers, and it was in my interest to get through them as fast as I could, get paid, and get out. An extra second or two on each ball could extend the evening by half an hour. The players liked it when I was slow, but those of us who worked there didn't.

The crowd reacted badly to sudden shifts in tempo. My trick was to shorten the time between balls slowly so the players could barely notice. I'd finally hit the point when someone yelled, "Slow down," and I then backed off a second or so between calls and hit the sweet spot where I could escape as fast as possible without getting mobbed by an angry crowd wielding their ashtrays. I knew of bingo callers who'd been booed off the stage, and once the police had come down to escort out a bingo caller who'd gone a little crazy and called numbers faster and faster until the customers swarmed him.

Bingo was the poor man's Las Vegas, and I was the closest thing that came to the spangled crooner. I was the king of the concrete banquet hall on the outskirts of Mississauga, a vast new suburb half-mud and half-crescent roads with names like Pony Trail.

That grubby level of celebrity had not been good enough for Ray, the predecessor who'd trained me. Ray had called bingo five nights a week for three years, always expecting a radio producer in the audience to pick him to host some show by virtue of his smooth, deep voice. Ray had his sights set high on three stations — pop hits at CHUM 1050, adult contemporary at CFRB, or even, who knew, Canada's national network, the CBC, from which it would be a hop skip and a jump to TV.

All the players below dreamed of hitting the bingo jackpot, and Ray up onstage dreamed of his voice going far beyond the church hall. He hoped for too long and then became bitter and quit in disappointment and rage and was sulking in his parents' suburban basement, still half-expecting a call.

I had different expectations. I was a parking lot attendant by day and a bingo caller by night. I was saving money because I had big plans outside the bingo hall. And I was a reasonably responsible parking lot attendant, one who didn't skim excessively off the top. I was in by eight sharp in the morning, and that meant I wanted to be out of the bingo hall by eleven if I could manage it.

That's why Bruno was watching me so closely.

I held my pace for a while and then Bruno walked away into the back room. I was feeling mischievous and was starting to crank the speed a bit when I glanced down in front of me and got a look from Gabriel, one of the regulars. Never Gabe, always Gabriel. Although he was scruffy with an unkempt short beard and long sideburns, he was fastidious about his name.

Gabriel and his wife, Angie, and her mother, Carol, were my bingo friends. We'd play a round of euchre if I ever arrived early at the hall. There usually wasn't much fraternizing between staff and customers. The ushers were mostly students and the managers were all Lithuanian church deacons, playing heavies for the sake of parish finances. The customers were working class. Radio producers didn't go to bingo games. Gabriel and Angie always sat front and centre and they came every single Thursday night. When Carol had a heart attack and was away for six weeks, I bought a rose for her on her return and they seemed to appreciate the gesture.

Gabriel's look up at me was important. "You're pushing it," the look said. "Slow down."

I eased off a bit and decided to give the crowd a break, and I drifted along in my eight-seconds-between-calls imagination, keeping a sharp ear for a bingo shout from the audience, but living an alternate life in my mind: a kind of highlights reel of Western culture with music, art, literature, and philosophical insights. I was imagining my version of bingo dreams when Carol in front of me called out the word.

We were playing the big game of the night, worth five hundred dollars, and she had been the only one to call so if the numbers were right, she was in the money for the full amount.

Carol had had a coronary and was flustered about being flustered, afraid for her poor heart. Angie double-checked her mother's card. Sometimes old people got the numbers wrong. But, no, the usher called back the numbers and I confirmed them, and Carol looked to her daughter and son-in-law with triumph. She may have had a heart attack, but she was back, and she was a winner.

Every night after the games were over, the senior management met in the kitchen of the hall to kill a bottle brought in by Father Peter, the old-school pastor who ran the parish like a well-managed farm. The senior management consisted of half a dozen of Bruno's cronies, all deacons in the church and of a certain age. I was the only young person because there was a bingo hierarchy and ushers were not invited for drinks. As caller, I had the privilege of having half a tumbler of random liquor and Coke with the men before rolling home. The liquor we were given depended on what the parishioners had given to Father Peter that week, often from wives cleaning out the liquor cabinets in an effort to reform their alcoholic husbands.

Gabriel was waiting for me outside the door.

"Hey, big win tonight for Carol," I said. "What are you going to do with the money?"

"Get in the car. You'll find out."

There was a taxi idling a little way down from the front door.

"That's great," I said, "but I'm working tomorrow."

"So am I. You won't regret it. Get in the car."

I was used to aggressive hospitality because Eastern Europeans employed it all the time. There was no defence against aggressive hospitality. If someone wanted you badly enough, you had to go along.

Angie was in the middle of the back seat and Carol was against the door behind the driver. Gabriel got in the front. Mother and daughter were sipping from a mickey of rye they had bought from the driver, and they passed it to me and told me to make it quick so Gabriel could get in a drink before we hit the road. The cabbie didn't want any cops seeing Gabriel drinking as he drove along. Gabriel drank and then turned to pass the bottle back, and when he did, he saw that Angie had put her hand on my leg. He laughed.

"My wife is grateful," he said.

"What's the plan?" I asked.

"We'll drop off Carol. She's still recovering from her heart attack, so she needs her rest, then the three of us will do a night on the town."

Carol took another sip of whisky and lit up a cigarette. Her recovery seemed to be going pretty well.

They all got out of the car when we arrived at their high-rise apartment, and it took Angie and Gabriel a long time to come back. The cabbie didn't say much. The meter was ticking happily away and I was his hostage in the back, assuring payment.

"Where are we going?" I asked when Angie and Gabriel came back down in party clothes.

"For a drink."

"Kind of late for that, but we might make last call." The bars in Toronto closed early in those days.

"Just you wait."

We drove half an hour to get downtown and into the old garment district. It had four- and five-storey warehouses that had seen better times. Half of the buildings were empty as the garments were starting to be made in other, cheaper countries, or else in industrial units somewhere past the edge of town.

"Drop us here," said Gabriel. We were on King Street at an alley between two warehouses. Gabriel and Angie seemed to know their way around. They led me down the unlit alley and turned a dark corner, where I saw the end of a lit cigarette.

"Shoes, man," a voice said. I couldn't even see the bouncer except in the glow from the cigarette end. How could he see my shoes? They were called Hush Puppies, soft suede shoes with crepe soles. Not exactly the footwear of the night-crawling bohemian class.

Angie and Gabriel led me out of the alley.

"I should've noticed that myself. Your shoes are no good," said Gabriel. "We'll never get in anywhere while you have those on."

"What's wrong with my shoes?"

"You look like a dork or an undercover cop."

He hit me in my soft spot. I'd grown up tall, gangly, and goofy, with eyeglasses and poor coordination, a sports disaster. I'd taken up smoking when I was seventeen and grown a beard to improve the image. I thought I'd succeeded.

"It's too late to buy new shoes," said Angie. "We could give him cab fare home."

They were going to ditch me. "Wait a minute," I said. It was a very warm night. I took off my shoes and stuffed my socks inside, and then set them in the small gap behind a dumpster in the alley. I had tough feet. The concrete barely registered under my soles.

Angie laughed. "That might do it, but we can't go back in that place. We'll have to go somewhere else. Watch out for broken glass."

We walked along the sidewalk and my feet were fine as long as I was careful. My feet were leathery anyway after a summer spent mostly barefoot. It turned out there were a lot more places we could try, and Gabriel and Angie seemed to know them all. I didn't know how they knew this kind of information. I didn't even know what their jobs were.

We walked down another alley, and Gabriel took the lead, holding his Zippo lighter in his hand so he could see if there was any glass on the way. This time we passed the heavy at the door.

The stairs up to the loading dock were made of some kind of spiky corrugated metal that bit at the soles of my feet. Gabriel opened the wooden gate in front of the freight elevator, then pulled the strap so the two doors opened up like jaws, and we got in.

"What is this place?" I asked.

"A booze can."

"What's that?"

"An after-hours bar."

The regular bars were still open, but I guess they wanted a longer commitment. I was a Boy Scout in Babylon.

In the light of the freight elevator, I could see their clothes were better than what they'd worn to bingo. Angie had on a short purple party dress, and Gabriel had an open-necked shirt in a swirly pattern.

The door opened into a very big room, the whole top floor of an old warehouse with wooden posts. Half a dozen televisions were hanging from the ceiling, each playing the same *Betty Boop* cartoon. Couches and ottomans were scattered throughout the room. Everybody was smoking. There was a long bar to one side where Gabriel got us drinks, and then we joined a half dozen people at one of the lounge areas. Some of them seemed to know Gabriel and Angie.

"Who's this?" a woman asked, pointing toward me with her jaw. She was wearing a tight grey dress, a little shiny. Her name was Jackie.

"Our bingo caller."

"The Barefoot Bingo Caller," Jackie said.

It was a quiet moment, and the phrase seemed to catch people's attention.

"Hey, Barefoot," some guy said, "give us a bingo call. Say 'Under the B, fifty-two.'"

"There is no fifty-two under the B," I said. "Fifty-two lies under the G."

"We have an expert," said Jackie.

"Oh, he's good, all right," said Angie. "Some of the ladies come to our bingo just for the sake of his voice."

"His voice isn't bad," said Jackie. She was watching me closely. She was pretty, in her late thirties, and she had eyes that stayed on me. I felt like I needed to perform.

"Under the G, fifty-two," I said in the deepest, roundest voice I could muster.

"Do you know where there's a fifty-two under the B?" asked Jackie. "At the bar. Gabriel, get us a round of B-52s and I'll pick up this one."

I didn't even know what a B-52 was. It turned out it came in a big shot glass, a layered drink, three kinds of sweet.

Everyone threw theirs back, and I did the same. When Jackie slipped away to the bathroom, I asked Gabriel who this Jackie was.

"They call her the queen of the booze cans. She has some kind of hotshot job, but she doesn't need much sleep."

"What kind of hotshot job?"

"Nobody knows."

We had developed some kind of crew around us. It reminded me of high school. There were a lot of beautiful women, and when I went to the bar to pick up a round, paid for by Gabriel, one of them started to comb my hair from behind. I turned to face her with the drink in my hand, and she smiled at me. She was very beautiful, made up like a high-fashion model.

"Will I see you later?" she asked.

"Sure," I said, and then carried my drinks back to the place where Gabriel and Angie and Jackie were sitting. I told Gabriel about the friendly woman at the bar.

"Hooker," he said. "If you want, I'll front you fifty, but you'll have to put up the rest yourself."

I said I'd pass.

"What's with the bare feet?" Jackie asked. I'd had a few drinks by this point and felt I could improvise.

"Ever hear of Shoeless Joe Jackson?" I asked.

"The baseball player. Sure. He played barefoot."

"Right. I'm a bingo caller who does his work barefoot."

"How does that make sense?"

I shrugged. Our crowd was loving it.

"Don't you hurt your feet?"

"They're very tough. Watch this."

I had a party trick that I'd sometimes pull in the summer when my soles were hard. I pulled on my cigarette, which was near the end anyway, and I looked around. I had everyone's eyes. I dropped the cigarette butt on the floor and then ground it out with the ball of my foot.

I guess it made an impression.

Jackie asked me to dance. Four or five couples were swaying in an open space, but she held me in her arms. I was pretty involved with someone else, but I guessed dancing with a beautiful older woman wasn't a crime.

After a while, I had to go to the bathroom. There was quite a line and it was mixed, which seemed friendly and normal to me at that point, even though unisex bathrooms were a couple of decades in the future. But it was an awfully long wait. After a while, one man and two women came out, and a couple went in. I waited, but gave up. When I got back, Jackie was awaiting me.

"Come on," she said.

"Where to?"

"I like you. We're going on a tour."

Gabriel shook hands with me before I left, and he palmed me a fifty-dollar bill.

It turned out to be a Toronto booze-can tour. Each of the places was different, from a few rooms above a store in Chinatown to some kind of artist's loft uptown to a place full of people all moving to some proto-techno music. The whole time I had to watch out for my feet. They weren't as tough as I'd made them out to be. A sharp object in the instep and I'd be crippled. Jackie and I rode around in cabs. Counting my twenty from calling bingo, I had seventy dollars in all, and it didn't go very far. Jackie didn't do cocaine, but cabs and entry fees and drinks ate up my cash. She didn't seem to mind. She picked up when I ran out. Sometimes Jackie would neck with me in the back of the cab, and I didn't take that too seriously either. She certainly didn't. When we got to a new booze can, she might wander off on her own, and I'd end up with a new crowd, pulling my cigarette butt trick a couple more times.

Just before dawn, we were in a place that got busted by the police. We were herded outside, but it didn't look like mere customers ever got charged. We had a hard time finding a cab because the hookers were finished for the night and their pimps had them in small herds, hailing the few cabs around. Jackie took me up Spadina just ahead of one such herd, and we stole a cab and then drove off as three women in slinky dresses and one man gave us the finger.

The cab pulled up in front of a small Victorian house on Belmont Street. The morning light was just coming up. Jackie paid for the cab and we stepped onto the sidewalk.

"What's this place?" I asked.

"My house. Are you coming in?"

I looked at my watch. "I start work in half an hour."

She shrugged. She dug in her purse and pulled out a business card. "Give me a call sometime," she said. And she turned and walked to her door. No goodbye kiss. No goodbye at all.

The parking lot wasn't all that far away. I started to walk.

It was a whole new world in the morning. People were going to work and some of them would look at my feet. They were very dirty, and they were sore. In the locker room at work, I found a pair of rubber boots. They were tight, but at least they covered my feet. I punched in and walked down to the parking lot shack. Once I got inside, I leaned my chair back against one wall and set my booted feet against the other wall until I was balanced just right. I crossed my arms and hunched over and anyone passing by in a car would think I was looking outside. Then I closed my eyes.

I awoke with a start. I'd been sleeping for maybe an hour, but I didn't feel refreshed. I hiked up to the cafeteria to buy a couple of coffees and one of those small packets of aspirins. When I paid for them, Jackie's card came out of my wallet. I had no intention of calling her, since I was involved with somebody else, but I read the card anyway.

Jackie Church, it said. Executive radio producer at the CBC.

THE SHACK

After I graduated from university I worked for my brother as a headhunter. Some hopefuls talked too loudly, some had drinking problems, and some wore jackets too bold for the pharmaceutical industry. There was one applicant who wouldn't look me in the eye, so I slowly rolled my chair into his line of vision, only to have him snap his head to look to the other side of the room. Out of curiosity, I slowly rolled my chair back into his line of vision only to have him look away again. After three months, I had learned a great deal about human nature, mostly my own. I was no good at this. I had earned not a single commission, so I took a full-time job at St. Michael's College as an attendant in a parking lot down the drive from St. Basil's Church on Clover Hill.

My father told his friends that I had done so well in school that the university had offered me an administrative job upon graduation.

Even an old high school chess club buddy was mortified when he saw me at this job. I found his stolen wallet on the lawn outside the parking shack. The money was gone but the ID was still there, and when I called him, he came to pick it up driving a new Firebird. I opened the small sliding glass window of the shack and passed the wallet out to him. For all he knew, maybe I was the one who had taken the cash in the first place.

The lot was for students and faculty and some of the regular Catholics who came to Mass at midday, so I didn't accept money — all I had to do was wave in the regulars and explain to others they couldn't park in my lot. It was a good place to sit down and get paid as I learned how to write.

"Keep your eye out for the cars parked up the hill," Father Iversen had said when he hired me. "Every couple of years, somebody forgets to put theirs in park, and one of them comes rolling down toward the shack."

"Couldn't you put up a metal post or something?" I asked.

"Don't tell me how to do my job. And what's with the decorations? It looks like a Polynesian whorehouse in here."

The Basilian teaching priests at St. Michael's were ascetics, aesthetes, or jocks. Father Iversen was among the latter. The booth faced south and had big windows and the direct sunlight was a killer, so I'd pasted up black construction paper on the upper part of the windows, and then Scotch-taped pictures from a calendar of German romantics to vary the field. Caspar David Friedrich's *The Wanderer above the Sea of Fog* was the central one. It didn't look Polynesian to me.

St. Michael's was the easternmost college of the University of Toronto, neo-Gothic academic buildings and a shady street with old houses gathered around St. Basil's Church. Across the street from my shack was an infirmary for retired priests. My shelter had a counter, a space heater, my chair, and a spare one for guests. Sin city, Toronto's Yonge Street, was just a couple of blocks away.

"You could live at home and save a lot of money!" my father

said, but I was dying to get out of Weston and out of my parents' house. Their expectations weighed on me. The small-town-turned-suburb where hockey was king had no future for me. I was hungry for literature and art, cars and noise and movie houses showing European flicks. When I packed up some boxes to move into my new apartment, my father stood on the driveway and said, "I remember bringing you home from the hospital. And now this." My mother was holding back her tears. I had to get away as fast as possible.

I moved into a second-storey room and kitchen in the Annex on Elgin Avenue. Down below on the ground floor, the retired Dr. Chong often stood on the porch smoking ciga-rettes. I shared the bathroom with a reclusive old woman who stole any toilet paper I left there. A young American philoso-phy professor lived one floor above us. He often had the local teenage girls visit him in packs up in his room. He said he was educating them and no one thought his kindness was unusual at the time.

Every day I'd walk fifteen minutes down to the university campus, punch in at the mailroom, and spend the rest of the day on display in a glass box like a specimen in a petri dish.

I spent most of the time daydreaming.

I watched the students going to class every day, and I knew a lot of them because I had just graduated the year before. My shack became a kind of clubhouse for my old poker buddies, and sometimes we squeezed a foursome game into the tiny space, but two of the players had to stand.

To the support staff, I was another slumming graduate, a tourist in their lives, but the gardeners were good to me, offering geranium roots that I was instructed to hang upside down over the winter and replant in the spring. I had no place to replant them and I didn't know where I'd be in the spring, but I took them home out of respect. Larry the street cleaner stopped by every weekday morning around ten. He carried a beer in his pocket and needed someplace to drink it.

I'd shaken loose my past and was ready to charge into my future. I was downtown and on my own in a job that paid me to sit at a counter and do whatever I wanted all day long, and my plan was to write, write, write and to save money for a trip that would take me farther away still. Australia was the most distant place I could think of, so I focused my dreams on that, although I had no clear idea of what I would do after I arrived.

The chronic care priests stayed on the fourth floor of the building across the way. Sometimes, one of them would stare out the window at me and I would stare back. The squirrels knew me and begged shamelessly, and while the weather was fine the cruel wasps buzzed in through my open window. I read a lot, and so when work was over and I went home, I didn't feel like reading anymore. I took apart the greasy old gas stove in the kitchen and cleaned all the parts. I walked the neighbourhood up and down. It had once been filled with rooming houses, but the old places had fine bones under the scum and now they were being gentrified.

I would get home from my walk and find it was still too early to go to bed.

My father was an occasional boozer who couldn't keep a bottle in the house overnight, so I took great pride in keeping a bottle of Canadian Club and another of Captain Morgan on my bookcase. I'd make myself a double with water or ginger ale, and then sit by the window, smoking cigarettes and looking outside. Not much happened on my street. When the squirrels stopped running around the leafy branches, I'd go out into the hall and around the corner to my kitchenette, rinse out my glass, and then turn in.

One of the younger students I knew was Snaige, the sister of someone I'd known from childhood summers at Wasaga Beach, where both our parents had summer cottages.

She had very bright eyes — everyone remarked on them and seemed to be attracted by them. She smiled easily and often and, as a result, she was usually in the company of other students. She'd wave at me as she passed the shack, but none of the others in her posse did. They were admirers, after all, and weren't eager to have any more competitors joining the pack.

The only time I ever saw her alone was in the mornings. She got off the Bay Street bus at the end of St. Joseph and had to walk past my shack. I'd say hi and she'd smile back, but she was usually in a hurry. She carried a big, flat suitcase.

I'd never seen one like it before. I didn't know very much about artists. They were exotic to me, not the sort of people you would find in Weston. The only artists I'd ever seen were in movies and the only artwork I'd seen beyond the woodland scenes on our walls at home was in the Time Life art books my mother bought. She hadn't bought them all, but we had Michelangelo, Rubens, Rembrandt, and Winslow Homer.

My art collection came from the stationery store. I'd get expensive art calendars in February when the prices were knocked down low and cut out the artwork to hang on my walls. I wished I knew more about art. I'd tried music in high school and been a terrible failure. I'd loved studying literature, but I was still hungry for more culture, and the sight of the big leather case she carried made me hungrier still.

"So what's in the bag?" I asked one day when she was going by. It was a warm fall day, and I had my chair set outside the shack.

"It's called a portfolio. Just some of my sketches from life drawing class."

"Can I take a look?"

"They're just sketches."

"Still."

She hesitated, but agreed. It was a little windy so we moved into the booth and she opened up her portfolio on my counter. It contained many sheets of newsprint with charcoal sketches of nudes, both male and female. Sometimes there were just parts of bodies — heads, or arms.

I nodded and listened as she spoke about speed and catching life in the line, things her profs had said to her. I felt I needed to be very quiet in order not to betray my ignorance. I was shy about looking at nudes with a woman, but I knew it was stupid. Back in Weston, the men would have sniggered at what she was showing me and, although I hated that part of my past, it was still a part of me. Maybe if I looked long enough and listened hard enough, that part of me would go away.

"What are you looking at?"

Her posse had arrived — Tom and James and Robin. Two of them crammed themselves into the booth unasked, and Robin waited outside.

"There's a new show opening at the Hart House Gallery," said Robin, and he convinced her to go there to see it before her next class.

She waved merrily at me as she left with them.

They were all students whose timetables were fixed only by their classes, which they might skip. But I was tied down to the spot in my shack. I couldn't follow her. I had only the morning moments as long as the posse didn't show up.

I would wait to see her getting off the bus a little before nine, and she'd wave to me from far away, knowing I was watching for her.

"Look at this," she said one day. It was getting cooler toward the end of October and now she always came into the booth. I liked to think she timed her arrival to give her a few extra minutes with me on her way to class. If the space heater had been running for a while, she took off her jacket and set it on the back of my guest chair.

This time, she opened an art book she had borrowed from the library to a painting by Paolo Uccello depicting the Battle of San Romano. In the painting of knights on horseback, the vast majority of the knights held upright lances, but two of the knights on the left of the painting had them half-lowered, as if pointing toward an enemy attack beyond the border of the image.

"What's important," she said to me, "is not just what's visible. The battle is about to begin, you see, but the action is going to take place in the future, beyond the frame of the piece. So the painting does two things. It shows the army, and then it leaves you to imagine the rest. In other words, the balance of the picture is implied in your mind."

"And who's the leader in the centre?" I asked, putting my finger on the man wearing a large hat.

"That," she said, putting her finger beside mine so both

were touching, "is Michele Attendolo, who led the Florentines in the battle against the Sienese. The man on horseback behind him has hair a lot like yours."

"My hair's too long," I said.

"I can cut hair."

"You can? Would you cut mine? I'll make you dinner if you do."

"Sure."

She was easy and friendly, just doing a favour for another from her pack of friends.

I didn't even know exactly where Siena was.

※

My kitchenette was very small and Snaige needed to squeeze past me as she trimmed. This brushing past me, and the touch of her fingers on my head as she worked her scissors, awoke something in me. I had wanted her to be a friend, and I had wanted to see her as often as I could, and the haircutting request had been made in innocence. But now my innocence was over.

When she had finished, I swept up the hair on the floor and put an awful homemade pizza in the oven. We drank wine in my room as we waited for it to bake. We drank more wine as we ate it, and I talked a great deal about my plans for Australia in the spring.

"Why do you want to go to Australia?"

"To see things. To get out of here. Everybody needs to escape the box they were born into." I was very committed, very intense.

She had a slight smear of tomato sauce on her cheek as she sat on the couch beside me, and I reached forward to brush it off. And then I kept going and I kissed her.

"Oh," she said. She was surprised, maybe even a little shocked. I had just been one of the posse, a friend. But now this.

She seemed a bit confused but then said, "You're going away to Australia in a few months."

"Yes."

That seemed to make it OK. She let me kiss her again.

After that, we saw a lot of each other. We always tried to get away somewhere private. Snaige worked part-time at the St. Michael's library, just down the street. It was quiet on Sundays, and on her break we went downstairs to sit together under the staircase.

"I'm beginning to be sorry you're going to Australia next year," she said.

⋊

It got dark earlier now and I hadn't turned on the overhead lamp or the desk lamp I kept on the counter while Snaige and I were in the shack. Still, we must have been visible because the phone rang. It was the old lady who ran the college switchboard up at the administration building beside the church.

"Look out the window," she croaked at me. She was a nice lady, but she had a rough voice from a lifetime of cigarettes. "What do you see?"

I didn't see anything.

"Look up at the infirmary windows."

I saw the dark outline of a man with the light behind him.

"Old Father Burns doesn't have much between the ears anymore, but he can still see, and he says you should cut it out."

"Cut what out?"

"I think you know what I mean."

We disentangled. We put an art book up on the counter. I turned on the overhead light and we were two students, studying a book side by side.

※

Snaige did not come by the booth for a long time. When I phoned her house, her parents said she was out. When I looked for her at the library, she'd taken some time off work. With not much else to do in the evenings, I walked around the city. It was a cold fall, and I'd go into the Coffee Mill Hungarian café, where the goulash was cheap and a violinist or a keyboard performer played a lot of Liszt. Sometimes I went to a café called Hazelton Lanes. There I drank jasmine tea for the first time and watched the skaters on artificial ice in the open courtyard on the other side of the glass wall. Forever after, I associated jasmine tea with melancholy.

※

I found Snaige outside the art building. She was carrying her portfolio and talking to Robin. Even with his winter coat on, I could see he was broad at the shoulders.

"Do you have time for a cup of tea?" I asked.

"Not really."

"There's a beautiful new café up in Hazelton Lanes. They serve jasmine tea and you can watch the skaters through a window."

"I have to get home."

"You've been avoiding me."

Most of her posse were insensitive to subtleties, but Robin caught the drift and disappeared.

"I haven't. Just that things were getting a little serious and, anyway, I've had a change in plans."

My mind raced over the members of her posse as I tried to determine which one of them had stolen her away.

"I'm quitting school at the end of this term."

It flashed through my mind that she was getting married. I felt a pang that made it hard to speak.

"What for? You'll only have a three-year degree if you do that. I thought you wanted to be an art teacher. You'll need four years for that."

"I've had a change of plans."

"So what are you going to do?"

"I've applied to the École des Beaux-Arts in Paris. I'll go over at the beginning of the summer and live with a French family, and then I'll start classes at the end of September."

"Why Paris?"

"Look, you were planning to go away anyway, and now I'm planning on going away. Why not Paris? I've got to go."

Now she was the one who was leaving, and she seemed to be cauterizing her heart in preparation for her departure.

⊠

Parents demanded their due, and I paid mine by spending a lot of weekends with them. But it was hard to be with them. My father wanted me to move back in and my mother wouldn't stop talking about law school. Snaige still lived at home and commuted to school. She let slip she was going up to the family cottage at Wasaga Beach with her father because she needed time to be alone.

I was sitting around with my parents after dark on Saturday evening when I turned to my mother and said I was going to drive up to Wasaga Beach.

Mothers have sensors. She knew something was going on. Our cottage was seasonal, freezing in the winter and just barely warm enough to be bearable in late autumn. She said she'd go too, and I didn't see how I could refuse. My father thought we were crazy to be starting out at night to a cold cottage. He decided to stay home to watch the hockey game.

It was a couple of hours' drive, and there were no other cars on the secondary highways once we got off the 400. I could keep my high beams on, and they formed a tunnel of light into the darkness.

Parents were dangerous. You couldn't tell them too much or they'd try to make you see things their way. And mothers were more dangerous than fathers because you couldn't fight them.

We didn't usually talk about relationships in our house, but now I talked about Snaige. It helped to be in the dark, where I couldn't see my mother, and I let it all pour out.

My mother was quiet for a while after I was done. Then she started to talk too, but not exactly in the way I expected. She talked about studying chemistry in university during the war. There was a young man in some of her classes, a student her own age. He would sit with her at lunch and she liked him well enough but never thought much about him. It was wartime, and she never paid much attention to politics either. She studied for her classes and went out with groups of friends from time to time.

One day her lunchtime admirer told her he came from a very remote place in the countryside. The surroundings were mostly bogs, but his parents had a farm tucked deep in among them. He'd grown up practically alone and had wanted to get away from that god-forsaken place and get an education. But now the Soviets were arresting people and shipping them out. Nobody came back. He told her that if she ever felt the noose tightening, she should let him know and she could go to his parents' farm. She'd be safe there. Nobody would find her.

He told her about his parents' farm more than once. At the time, she didn't really pay much attention to him. He was just one of her gang. But in the decades since then, she thought of him often. She had thanked him, but thought he was overreacting.

Then one day he was gone, put into a cattle car by the Soviets and shipped away, and she never saw him again. It was very sad, but he was only one among many. Then the Germans came and, after a while, among other crimes, they were taking away single men to work in factories in Germany. Suddenly my mother had a whirlwind romance and a proposal from an older man who ended up being my father. This was followed by decades of bickering, with frequent explosions of temper and brief reprieves of calm.

If her admirer was trying to save her, what could she have meant to him?

"Did he have a name?"

She told me. It was the same as my middle name.

It was just before nine by the time we got to Wasaga Beach. I lit up the oil stove and left my mother in our place. It was windy and cold but there wasn't any snow on the ground, and I could hear the waves breaking at the beach a few blocks away.

When I drove up to Snaige's cottage, I saw the lights were on inside, so I knocked on the door.

Her father was surprised to see me. It was kind of late and hardly anybody was up at the beach at that time of year, yet he invited me to step in quickly to keep out the cold air. It was a small place with wood panelling and a kitchen sink and table at one end of the room and a couch and couple of armchairs at the other. The room smelled a bit of stove oil from the small Coleman furnace in the corner.

Snaige was wearing a ski sweater and sitting in a wicker armchair, and she looked neither happy nor unhappy to see me. She was cordial. She offered me tea and cookies and I accepted.

Her father was a genial man known for his goatee, considered eccentric at the time. He asked after my mother but he didn't ask what brought me by so late in the season and so late in the day. He was an amateur naturalist who talked for a while about the birds that overwintered in that part of the country and then about the varieties of local apples, some of which could be picked off the trees even after the frost. Snaige listened to him and didn't say much. I couldn't read her at all.

"I've been discussing my daughter's plans for the future," he said, "and maybe you could add your thoughts. She'd like to go to Paris to continue her studies, but her mother and I are concerned that she'll lose the chance to get into teachers' college and find a good job."

I lit a cigarette and reflected for a moment, and then began to talk slowly and thoughtfully. In my experience, it was not good to frighten off parents. You couldn't wax poetic or be too intense with them. You had to be serious, but not so serious as to set off their bullshit meters.

I explained how the market for art teachers in Toronto was very full, and a graduate of teachers' college without special qualification would have to go somewhere far north to get a job. On the other hand, the art school in Paris was famous. It had cachet. Anyone who studied art in Paris and then returned to do teachers' college would have the edge over anyone local. And, for that matter, I was considering taking the Foreign Service exam at some time in the future, but I had always been weak in French and might need to spend some time in France upgrading my language skills. Not Paris, though. I'd heard there were schools in Toulouse and Grenoble. But if Snaige were studying in Paris, I might drop by for a visit.

"You're planning on going to France?" Snaige asked.

"I'm pretty sure, yes."

"What happened to Australia?"

"I'm still on my way there in the long run. Paris is on the way, isn't it?"

※

When I got back to my parents' cottage, my mother was still up. We never travelled anywhere without food and drink, and she'd brought along some pizza dough and cheddar cheese and made buns while I was out. It was close to midnight, and the buns were still warm.

This uncanny ability of parents to know things, such as when I would return, was something I took for granted at the time. I would have been surprised not to find some kind of food and drink ready to go on the table whenever I arrived. She had also brought a small bottle of cherry brandy, which we sipped along with our tea as we ate the warm buns.

We didn't talk about Snaige. It was different now that we were sitting in the light. And it was embarrassing for a man, no matter how young, to have taken a tip on romance from his mother. Instead, I talked about Paris. What a wonderful city it was and how I regretted that I'd done so badly in French in high school.

1978-1983

BABYLON REVISITED

Ted Joans was a leftover beat poet who still came through Paris in the late seventies, a kind of relic who sold his own chapbooks and would tell you stories about Jack Kerouac if you took him out to dinner. It didn't have to be an expensive restaurant — he just wanted his big belly filled and the Vietnamese restaurant around the corner on Rue de la Bûcherie was fine. Apparently he had ten kids somewhere. I didn't know who filled their bellies.

Jack Belden was another regular. The toothless chain-smoking writer had been a war correspondent in China, walked out of Japanese-occupied Burma with Stillwell, had his left leg shattered while reporting close to the front in Italy, and then gone on to cover the invasion of Europe. He was writing poetry now instead of journalism. His fingertips and the ends of his shoulder-length white hair were yellow with nicotine stains. He was always hungry too, but he ate a lot of bread at every meal so it wasn't all that expensive to take him out. When his eyeglasses broke, he fixed them with Scotch tape.

Nancy Cole dressed all in black before that became fashionable, and her hair was coal black as well, cut at a sharp angle like something out of the twenties. She did one-woman shows of Gertrude Stein's work whenever she could raise the cash to rent out a theatre. She did this for twenty years and then disappeared on a bus trip to the American South. Nobody knew her well enough to go looking for her, and she never reappeared.

English literary Paris seemed to be in terminal decline and its bookstore, Shakespeare and Company, felt like a memorial instead of a pulsing heart.

Anglophone travellers and literary hopefuls like me bought their books at Shakespeare and Company. The bookstore was a warren of rooms overseen by the ageing, cranky self-proclaimed communist George Whitman. He was a wiry Ichabod Crane with straggly long hair that flopped over the left side of his head like a sliding toupee, and he smoked cigarettes using empty tuna tins as ashtrays. He drank his tea from glass yogurt containers.

English books were expensive, and the best value came in fat mass-market books that contained a lot of pages, so I read a lot of James Clavell and swore I'd never buy anything with fewer than three hundred pages.

I was looking for something in Paris and was having a hard time finding it. Shakespeare and Company was a museum to the kind of world I hoped to inhabit. Maybe I would have been better off somewhere else, but I couldn't leave Paris because Snaige was a student at the École des Beaux Arts and if I left her for any length of time, yet another posse might begin to form.

I saw a notice on the door the next time I went to buy a fat novel at the store. There was a new English literary journal called *Paris Voices*, and there was going to be a reading of its contributors on a Tuesday night.

So on that day I took the commuter train back into Paris after I finished work as an English teacher in Versailles. It was a smooth twenty-five-minute ride, and I was writing my short stories in those daily intervals.

I was always cold and hungry in Paris, but I still had enough to buy cigarettes. I was student-poor, not a pauper. It rained or dropped wet snow that melted on the sidewalk all winter long and my shoes leaked. I lived on the Arab potato and hot dog sandwiches served on heavy, deep-fried rolls shaped like jelly doughnuts.

I bought one of those sandwiches, heavy as half a brick, from a window in the Latin Quarter, empty now that tourist season was over, and went into the bookstore looking for Ken Timmerman, the editor of the journal. It was still early, and the bookstore had a scattering of travelling Americans and hangers-on from the American College. It was a warm place where you could linger. I didn't see a likely candidate around.

I went up the steep staircase, practically a ladder, which had a gate on it that said the upstairs was only open to library members. Everyone else seemed to ignore the sign so I did too. There were two big rooms up there as well as a squat toilet that doubled as a shower. One of the rooms contained a desk and a few office chairs as well as a couch in the middle of the book-lined walls. The other had a double bed and a big window that overlooked Notre Dame Cathedral, lit up now through the rain-streaked window.

A man around my age was sitting on the edge of the bed, reading a book. He was like a younger version of George

Whitman: thin, with thick reddish-brown hair and eyeglasses and a long beard like something out of the nineteenth century. He looked up at me.

"I'm looking for Ken Timmerman," I said. "Do you know what he looks like?"

"Keep away from Ken Timmerman," he said.

"Why?"

"He's an egotistical asshole."

"Do you know him?"

"A bit. He pisses off people."

"Okay then," I said. "I'll keep that in mind."

The speaker struck me as an egotistical asshole as well, but the place was full of them. Every young person who spoke English and wanted to be someone in Paris showed up at Shakespeare and Company, looking for a scene. We were literary hustlers without proven talent, but we wanted to be taken seriously on our promise alone, preferably fast. It turned out there was no scene.

Paris wasn't cheap anymore. It ate up the money of those of us who earned it, and it ate up the money of those of us whose parents sent it along in time-limited indulgence.

I bided my time in the store, read a little Lawrence Durrell, and then I went back downstairs to the reading where about thirty people had shown up. Ken Timmerman spoke first. He was the same man who'd warned me about Ken Timmerman upstairs.

Ken was rude, provocative, and energetic, and you were welcome to work with him or hang with him if you could take his maddening self-confidence and the plentiful insults he hurled at you to see if you could take them without crumbling.

It didn't hurt that he was a good cook. You'd stop by his two-room apartment and find him cooking jugged hare. He funded *Paris Voices* out of his own pocket and he welcomed anyone who would help work on it. "Welcomed" was not exactly the right word. "Tolerated" might have been closer to the mark.

I folded printed sheets into signatures for the printer, a Jew who carried a pistol because, in addition to printing our journal, he printed a magazine called *Israel and Palestine* that aimed at the reconciliation of the Jews and Arabs. Everyone wanted to kill him. I canvassed bookstores to carry the journal, and for this I and the rest of us were permitted to enter the world of literature in his "editorial collective," a precise description of a journal with a lefty literary bent.

Finally there was a scene, and the five of us on the collective were it.

Dan was a tall American with a French wife, and he was being nice to her by living in Paris for a while. Titus was a short, gravelly voiced Californian with tinted round glasses and a street lexicon. He was the first person I ever heard use the expression, "Say what?" He played the guitar as well as wrote poetry, and he was a buddy of Mark, an American southerner who learned to play the dulcimer. The two of them would eventually play for food on Greek islands.

Together, we tried to figure out what literature was. How to make it, how to read it, and how to tell the good from the bad.

This proved to be harder than we'd imagined. Ken admired John Hawkes, I liked Hemingway's short sentences, and Titus admired Allen Ginsberg. We all admired John Fowles and we wrote *Magus*-like stories in which sexually generous young women indulged cocky young men. The logo of the magazine was a satyr, whose erect penis reminded me of a compass needle that signified Ken's own penis. It pointed toward any available woman.

We met every week upstairs at Shakespeare and Company to read manuscripts and to read one another's work. We published ourselves, but it would have offended us to think that we were self-promoting. Instead, we honestly believed we were critiquing each other's work, and at times an editorial meeting felt like a cross between a communist reeducation camp and a therapy session. We held work to the highest standards but we were unsure what the measuring stick should be, except for distaste for all writing that was genre.

The trick was to give criticism that was couched in supportive terms.

"I'm not getting this," I might say.

The response could be contrite, or it might be aggressive.

"Try a little harder," the writer would reply.

Fathers loomed large in our writing, typically tyrants of one kind or another. Dan had been raised in a Catholic school and he hated nuns, some of whom met fiery deaths in his work. Our writing was often a form of revenge.

Sometimes we ran into aesthetic battles that divided us according to lines of friendship. None of us took criticism well, and some took it worse than others.

One afternoon we were in the upstairs front room of Shakespeare and Company, Ken sitting on the bed there beside a stack of manuscripts, and Dan, Mark, Titus, and I on chairs in a half circle facing him. Ken had just dropped off some criticism with Sam, a big Israeli army vet downstairs, and now we were trying to criticize a story by Titus.

"The passage where the father tells his son he is drinking too much is too long," I said. Actually, the passage was repetitive and interminable, like a lot of our writing at the time.

"Define too long," said Titus.

"Yeah, define it," said Mark.

"Too long is too long," I said. Ken was staying out of this. I was on my own.

"Too long is subjective," said Titus.

I was exasperated. "It's boring!" I finally said.

Titus beamed at me. "Mission accomplished!" he said. "I wanted to show that the son was bored by his father's tirades. If you were bored, you have echoed the son's emotional response."

Heavy footsteps came up the staircase around the corner and suddenly big Sam was there, as if representing all the fathers we had dissed in our work. He kept his hair short, military style, and he was wearing a leather jacket. In his left hand he held a crumpled sheaf of papers and with his right hand he reached forward and grasped Ken by the shirt front and pinned him back against the wall at the side of the bed.

"What's this about?" Ken squeaked.

"It's about your shitty commentary on my poems," he said. "You show no respect. You've ruined my writing day. Do you know what that means?" Ken was in shock. So were we.

Sam answered for him. "It means I've lost a day of writing. I'm upset, you understand? You've set me back."

"Sam," said Titus, "this crowd of pricks has set me back too. Let's ditch the morons."

"Timmerman has to pay," said Sam.

"Let him stew in his own shit," said Titus. "I can't write anymore today either. Come on, I'll buy you a drink."

"One drink won't do it."

"Then I'll buy a bottle of wine and we'll go to the park and get pissed."

Sam wavered.

"I need to get pissed," Sam said. "I need to wash away the taste of shit from my mouth."

Titus stood up. Sam glared at Ken and shook him, then let him go. Titus looked like a miniature version of Trotsky with his round tinted glasses, and Sam was as big as a storm trooper. They went out together.

"Do you think Titus saved the day because he's so smart, or do you think he was as angry at us as Sam?" Dan asked.

Ken shrugged.

"Are you OK?" I asked him.

He smirked. "They'll be back. No one else will even read their writing, let alone publish it. Let's look at the next piece."

※

We read manuscripts again and again. We ate together, buying a lot of cheap chicken livers and blood sausage. We drank *vin mousseux*, the inexpensive version of champagne, and we wrote and talked literature. We published a few writers who went on to make names for themselves — the Welsh poet Tony Curtis, the Irish novelist and playwright Sebastian Barry, and Garry Apgar, a cartoonist who went on to write about Disney and Mickey Mouse. Ken was unbearable but he was charismatic and had force: he became a left-wing intellectual and was the first one among us to publish a novel.

Snaige lived on the top floor of an unheated seven-storey walk-up on Rue de Paradis. Ominously, her landlady was named Madame Malivoire, which we translated very loosely as "Mrs. Evil-Seeing." True to form, when the family ate rabbit for dinner, she sent up the cooked head as a treat for Snaige.

Thinking I wanted independence, I lived halfway across town in the fifteenth district, but not for long. A new posse was forming around Snaige. On my way down the stairs after a late-night visit with her, I met Dr. Ken on his way up for an even-later-night visit. I went back up with him. After that, I had to get her to move in with me quickly to fend off the other suitors.

In a definitive move to get Snaige all to myself, I married her in the Église Saint-Paul-Saint-Louis in the Marais district. That July afternoon, as we walked back from the church along the crowded market-day sidewalk to the reception, the street vendors called out *"Vive les maries!"* and the wedding guests behind us were offered free strawberries from the heaping carts on the roadside.

Paris was over for us soon after that. We returned to Canada partly for the sake of my ageing parents and partly because I needed an English-speaking world in which to write.

※

But one returns to Paris after one has lived there, and the place is never the same. By the time we revisited Paris, I thought George would be dead but he was still there, drying like a prune in the chair at the front desk of Shakespeare and

Company, as he would for another twenty years. The store was full of people cut from the same cloth as we had been, still expatriates looking for a scene but with different sensibilities. I stumbled across a literary meeting up in the room where Ken Timmerman had been lifted by his shirt front five years before. A writer was talking, and I listened. He was dressed in a crewneck sweater and talking about his travel work for the Let's Go publishing group. As the only one in the room who made any money from writing, he was much admired. No one was talking about poetry or literature, as I understood it. The zeitgeist had turned commercial.

"I don't go there much anymore," said Ken. He had lost the beard and his short hair was receding slightly. He was still full of energy and was building a cabinet in his Paris apartment when I saw him. Ken always liked a crowd of people, and he survived by doing whatever he intended to do no matter who was around. I hadn't seen him in five years, but that didn't matter. He was building a cabinet.

He had a tall Swede named Christina in the apartment. Within half an hour of my being there, she told me she would cut off his dick if he fooled around. Ken didn't react to the statement. He was sanding a piece of trim and he kept doing it. He'd finally found a woman who could rein in his worst impulses.

"Why don't you go to Shakespeare and Company?" I asked.

"I don't write fiction anymore. It's insignificant to me. Now I write about politics in the Middle East."

He had decided to make a name for himself as a journalist, so he flew into Beirut in the spring of 1982, a PLO sympathizer out to write up the injustices of the war. But he only lasted a day or so. The PLO didn't buy his story and, worse, he had an American passport and a Jewish-sounding name. He was locked into a basement prison under an apartment building and there he rotted for weeks, never sure if he would be shot or used as a hostage of some kind. Then Israel invaded and started the seven-day siege of Beirut. In the days Ken was held in the basement prison, the top half of the apartment building was knocked off due to shelling. His guards grew edgy. They would point their weapons at him and say "bang" playfully, but not very playfully. One morning they were gone and later that day an Israeli soldier broke down the door and released Ken and two Frenchmen who had been imprisoned with him.

Ken went into that basement a bohemian fiction writer and came out a conservative, God-fearing Republican agitator. All of us had changed, but nobody else had changed so drastically in such a short time.

I became involved in a little journalism in the late eighties and early nineties when the Soviet Union was collapsing, and I always tried to fly through Paris, so I saw him once a year or so into the early nineties. Ken and Christina had a riotous blended family that Ken marshalled and drove mercilessly as he cooked, did the wiring in the house, did interviews about the Middle East, and drank heavily in the evenings. After dinner and when the children were in bed, Christina would sit on his lap and neck with him as we finished off the wine.

On the way upstairs to bed one night, he paused and showed me a French book in which he was named as an American operative of the CIA. He loved to provoke and he loved to hint, but he hated to be precise, so he never explained the truth. He writes on today from his home in Maryland, no longer the Ken Timmerman I knew at Shakespeare and Company.

But none of us is that person who sat upstairs at the bookstore with the view over Notre Dame, trying to figure out literature, and trying to figure out ourselves.

Karen Mulhallen sometimes took my phone calls from a bubble bath. In those days, Bell Canada forbade telephone jacks in bathrooms but Karen got one anyway. Whatever Karen wanted, Karen got. From the bath, she would direct me on the subscription list that I was delegated to run by virtue of my junior position on *Descant*. She ran the journal out of her flat at 19 Washington Avenue, the coolest place I had ever seen.

It had a baby grand piano, furniture made out of chrome tubes, and a painting on the wall the size of a dining room table. It depicted a babe, and Karen was something of a babe as well. She was like a collision between the body of Marilyn Monroe and the savvy of Sylvia Beach. Karen was a Blake scholar and like one of those high-strung intellectual women out of a Robert Stone novel, minus the cocaine habit and the revolutionaries.

Where was literature in Canada? It was hard for me, freshly back from Paris, to find a way to it. Karen took me in at *Descant*, a place where literature and bonhomie wrestled for supremacy. Literary Toronto had not fully formed yet. Down at Harbourfront, the dreary wind whistled through the old warehouse venue that had not yet been discovered by hipsters, tourists, literati, or even vagrants. It was cold and empty down

103

there. The room was vast and the audience was small. Parking was free. Most literary readings were attended by the author, the spouse, host Greg Gatenby, and three or four of us others in the audience. Afterward, we would go out for beers, and M.T. Kelly in his drinking days could be counted on to say things to the waitress that would get him arrested today.

We editors at *Descant* were a boozy, foodie crowd. We celebrated American Thanksgiving with a meal including sweet potato pie, Bastille Day with *cassoulet* and my Eastern European roots with herring and mushrooms. We drank every new liquor that began to appear on the liberalizing liquor store shelves. We were early adopters of Campari, followed by Suze, Pimm's, and mixtures such as kir. I was fond of Polish Zubrowka because Somerset Maugham had once published a paragraph in its praise and, besides, it was illegal in Ontario. Of wine there was an ocean.

And then there was the writing.

Over plates of tapas and glasses of rioja, we pored over mountains of slush pile submissions on Karen's dining room table. There was Russell Brown, a Canadian literature special-ist with great storytelling style and a booming voice, and his wife, Donna Bennett, quiet and understated as Russell was loud, but equally ironic — you just had to listen carefully. Gord Sato was a Bay Street lawyer who knew all the current Canadian writers and did literature for his amusement.

In my unformed literary mind, I yearned for a yardstick by which to judge submissions to *Descant*, and when my coedi-tors argued that I just needed to develop and apply my taste, I became frustrated. "What is it that you want?" Russell asked me. In my ardour, I said I wanted only submissions that burned.

At the same time I was writing stories and novels but most of my literary forays ended in disaster. Having written a novel about a train ride to the USSR, I found out that an old classmate of mine from St. Michael's College at U of T, Ed Carson, was now working as an editor at Stoddart Publishing. I sent him my manuscript and waited. Eventually, he called to say I should meet him at the Prince Hotel restaurant, a fashionable place in the east end of town near the publishing house.

I was nervous and I was excited. After all, it looked good. Why would Ed Carson ask me to lunch if not to publish me? Ed was a study in contrasts, a long-haired, bearded face in a sharp suit, a kind of hippie literary businessman. Anxious for my manuscript's future, I felt it was important not to make a bad impression.

When the waiter came through the crowd of starched tablecloths and businessmen, silver pen in hand, he told us, almost as an aside, that one of the specials was ravioli. This choice, I thought, would send the right message. I would eat unpretentious, earthy food. I ordered the ravioli.

As soon as the waiter left, Ed turned his beard to me and said, "The first thing I want to tell you is we are not going to publish this novel."

All I could think of was the damned ravioli, which I had ordered instead of the steak.

Ed Carson turned down that novel and another one, and there was no second restaurant invitation.

I felt as if I were trying to climb up a hill of sand. I could find no purchase, no way up. An editor at Lester & Orpen Dennys liked one manuscript so much, she encouraged me to take half a year off teaching to rewrite. I did that, and when

I went back to find her, she had left the firm, and no one else was interested. An editor at McClelland & Stewart kept the manuscript for a year and then mailed it back to me unread. She said she knew I would want it back.

But through all of this difficult time, I was sustained by *Descant* and the magnificent table heaped with items I had never imagined in my suburban youth — chocolate-covered espresso beans, homemade mayonnaise, olive oil in the perplexing grade of "extra virgin." And of course, the mountains of manuscripts.

Slowly, very slowly, literary journals began to accept my stories. Then I got a good break when a friend suggested I write a commercial article for a new general interest magazine called *Ontario Living*. Even there, I courted disaster by twice delivering five-thousand-word articles while editor Liz Primeau had asked for two thousand words. She did me a favour by calling me to her house on a Sunday afternoon. I didn't even realize I was getting a favour.

Elegant and businesslike, measured and calm, Liz Primeau chatted with me in a friendly way, and then brought out her steel. "Listen," she said calmly over tea, "deliver the two thousand words I asked for, or I'll get someone else to write the piece."

I listened. I wrote what she asked for, and she published it as the cover article in the magazine's launch.

She paid me two thousand dollars for that story, a vast sum at the time. At the magazine launch in a chic restaurant off Yonge Street near St. Clair, there were mountains of calamari, still novel at the time, an open bar, and a door prize of a wind surfer. I ate and I drank prodigiously, and I won the door prize.

Luckily, I had ski racks with me, so I put the wind surfer on the roof of my car and drove through light snow to the house of *Descant* coeditor Russell Brown. I rang his bell although it was well after eleven. He came to the door in a housecoat.

"Antanas," he said, "what are you doing here?"

In my cocktail elation, I replied that I had been paid two thousand dollars, been fed and watered, and given a wind surfer for my trouble. I pointed down the long steps across the vast lawn to my car at the curb and, upon it, a wind surfer covered with snow. I said I was ready to sell out literature for the rewards of freelancing.

But I wasn't, really. *Descant* was my home base, the place where I returned to trumpet my successes and to mourn my losses. In another extravagant meal, an echo of Woody Allen's *Annie Hall* of a few years earlier, we *Descant* editors decided to do a literary meeting late in the morning and then spend an afternoon making paella. By coincidence, this was to happen the day after I'd had a minor chest operation. We started with an editorial meeting while drinking Spanish Cava, and from there in mid-afternoon we moved to cooking. I ran out to Kensington Market to buy lobsters, one of which escaped briefly and huddled under the dining room table. I had brought my own apron to protect my pale blue shirt. As the day progressed, we moved to Pimm's and soda. Gord Sato drank only Scotch. It was a very hot day, and I could feel the sweat running down my back, indeed everywhere, but the mood was great. Spouses joined us later for dinner. We were at the peak of our hilarity, ready to sit at the table, when I took off my apron and sat down.

I had never been stared at by a whole tableful of people.

When I looked down, I saw that the stitches in my chest had broken, and my entire shirt front was covered in blood.

I expected sympathy, solicitousness, and first aid. But everyone was happy and hungry and when they saw I was not mortally wounded, Karen told me to go to the bathroom and soak the shirt in cold water. She also gave me a Band-Aid.

"Don't you have a shirt left behind by one of your boy-friends?" I asked.

She gave me a look. She could be withering when she chose. We had an obligation to literature and one to good fellowship as well. Did I intend my bloody shirt to dampen the festivities? I soaked the shirt in the bathtub, washed out the blood, put on the Band-Aid, and returned to the table. The shirt was indeed damp, but the festivities were not.

I went from shy and intimidated to cocky and opinion-ated. I could talk books all night. Anne Collins gave me my first print review to write in the *Globe and Mail*, and I did many for years after that, and then producer Richard Handler brought me into CBC Radio, where I worked sometimes with Shelagh Rogers and Richard in the warmest atmosphere I ever felt on air.

Soon Snaige and I had one son and then another, I taught English full-time at Humber College, and there was no time, but always I circled back to writing. I continued to write nov-els that went nowhere, although magazines were publishing my stories. And still I freelanced and edited and ate and drank at *Descant*.

Then came a hiatus of four years when politics overcame literature in my life. When the Soviet Union began to col-lapse, I had an in, due to my knowledge of Lithuanian, and the Lithuanian Soviet Socialist Republic was on the cutting edge of the collapse.

The impossible became possible, but my years of work as a writer and pundit for the cause of Soviet destruction had exhausted me. By the early nineties, I had left *Descant* and it looked as if I might as well leave literature for all the progress I had made.

But I couldn't *not* write, so I assembled yet another novel, my fourth, and in 1994 a small Canadian press agreed to publish it. At long last, pushing the age of forty-one, I was getting into print with a book. But I soon learned the striving and the comedy did not end with the publication of a book. The life of literature was not a high jump. It was a series of hurdles. To get a book published was one thing. To get anyone to notice was another.

And it almost didn't happen, due mostly to a single margarita, a drink I didn't favour under normal circumstances.

I was asked to interview visiting literary biographers for radio. In my capacity as interviewer/critic, I took a call from the publicist of Graham Greene's biographer, Michael Shelden.

"We're having a little reception for Mr. Shelden," she said, and named a good Toronto restaurant. "All the *crème de la crème* of the media will be there."

The dinner was to be an especially tricky assignment for me. My own novel was just out and everybody whom I wanted to review it would be in that room.

The eatery looked like a nineteenth-century grand French restaurant with all the modern amenities. We had two private rooms, one for drinks and the other for dinner. I ordered a margarita from the waiter.

The drink came in a martini glass the size of the Mediterranean. I needed two hands to hold it. It looked like a triple raised to the nth power. The size of the glass was making the wrong impression for this, the dawning age of abstinence. I did the only thing I could to get rid of it: I drank the margarita quickly.

My anxiety evaporated and seemed to take my good sense with it. I should have known I was tipsy when I started having a good time. Literary events were not necessarily about good times.

When dinner was announced, the guests fit into eight tables of eight each. I had enough reserve intelligence to realize that I'd better not try to be noticed in my present condition. Invisibility was preferable to making the wrong impression. And yet, Katherine Ashenburg, then editor of the books section of the *Globe and Mail*, was sitting two over on my right. She could be the career maker. I had to make a good impression.

The duck was excellent and the wine superb. A waiter kept topping up the glass whenever it got low. I noticed that Katherine Ashenburg did not eat her duck. She ate only the vegetables around it. This fact troubled me greatly. Wasn't a duck a good thing? Shouldn't every roast duck be consumed?

Michael Shelden's biography of Graham Greene turned out to be a big hit because it went straight for the throat. It was the kind of biography that made Woody Allen's reputation look saintly. Shelden spoke before taking questions, laying out the alleged sins of Greene. These were many. The wine was frightfully good, and it did not stop coming throughout Shelden's speech.

And I continued to look at the uncleared duck cooling on the plate of Ashenburg. It would be great to have the *Globe and Mail* review my book, but the sight of the duck was making me lose all sense of proportion.

Was half a duck worth a literary career? Maybe not. But I was beginning to understand Esau, who had sold his birthright for a bowl of pottage. Whatever pottage was, it could not be as good as duck. As the brilliant Sheldon moved through his testimony as witness for the prosecution, I half-rose with fork in hand to reach over my dinner table neighbour and spear the duck off the plate of unsuspecting Katherine Ashenburg. Did heads turn? Perhaps. Had I blown my chances? Most probably. But with the exuberance I had learned at *Descant*, I sawed through the carcass, fully in the knowledge the cold half duck might turn out to be the sum of my literary reward.

TOWN *and* COUNTRY

When I married Snaige in Paris, I thought it would be useful for us to establish a few life rules to avoid misunderstandings.

"When we take vacations," I said, "my version of the ideal holiday is a hotel lobby with big reading chairs, plenty of newspapers and ashtrays, and a waiter who will bring drinks from the bar."

"I agree," said Snaige, by which she meant her idea of a perfect vacation was getting into a canoe, paddling long distances, and sleeping in a tent on rocky ground. This wasn't the only version of her ideal vacation. Another was walking long distances on uneven paths along poorly marked trails.

While we lived in France, we didn't really have to think about our preferences too much. We'd get invited to the country houses of our friends' parents, where we might sit under fragrant laurel trees and drink Ricard, or take a basket and walk a hundred yards up the hill to buy chèvre from the farmer next door.

So far, so good.

But when we returned to Toronto, there was a distinct lack of laurel trees and local cheesemakers. There was always Wasaga Beach, where we had grown up summering, but we had taken on a little *hauteur* about that place. Wasaga Beach was about greasers and hamburgers, rye and ginger ale, and too many of our parents' old friends who wanted to know when we were going to have babies. As for me, I was unemployed and that meant there would be no hotel lobbies for us to holiday in any time soon.

Reluctantly, I had the countryside thrust upon me, a bookish former suburbanite with literary and European pretensions.

※

When my brother bought an old farm in Grey-Bruce County, the whole family pitched in to help him build his frame house. A dozen fractious relatives hammered by day and got hammered by night. My father was too old to climb a ladder anymore but he could still explain clearly, loudly, and at length what we were doing wrong from his place down on the ground. The house was far from the road, so there was no electricity, the generator boomed, and we hauled in water from the river. Over three days we had the shell built.

Grey-Bruce County is hilly farming country that broke the hearts of generations of farmers who cleared the land of cobblestones every spring only to have new ones rise up again next season. Somehow, they managed to farm the land with horses until World War II, but the tractors could never take the steep hills and the land wasn't really worth putting much money into. Near Priceville, on the back roads, the countryside felt like a European landscape that had been emptied of people. Most of the fences still stood, and some of the fields still brought in hay crops to the few remaining farmers, but, for the most part, hawthorn and sumac were covering the fields that were cleared with so much sweat about a hundred and fifty years before.

Snaige and I went up together to do a little finishing once the rough work was done. Snaige is an artist, and she could be counted on to do the finer work, such as putting caulking around the windows without leaving great globs that might drip and end up like dry, hard tears suspended by threads from the window frame.

When darkness fell, we played gin for a while by the oil lamp, and then unfolded the slippery vinyl couch. She was wearing a long cotton nightgown with a few frills around the neck — something that pioneer women would have recognized as suitable nightwear for the Canadian wilderness. The couch sloped gently away to both sides from the centre, and we kept sliding off the edges, but we finally found more or less permanent positions and went to sleep.

The sound that awoke us was enough to drive any civilized person permanently downtown. Something, probably a large beast by the sound of it, was eating the house. The place had no interior partitions yet, and the uncanny sound of something gnawing on wood echoed through the place.

"What's that?" she asked. "A bear?"

"No, bigger."

It did not seem likely that a moose could be gnawing on the house. Teeth scraped against the wood repeatedly.

"Let's just lie here quietly, and maybe it'll go away," I said.

Snaige said nothing. We waited about fifteen minutes, an eternity in the dark.

"I can't sleep," she said.

"Neither can I."

"You'll have to chase it away."

I had never been called on to do anything like that back in Paris.

I girded myself for battle. I put on my jeans and workboots, shirt, jacket, and hat, then thought better of it and put on a sweatshirt as well. I reasoned that the thicker my clothes, the less deeply the claws of the animal would cut into my flesh. I carried a flashlight in one hand and a log roller in the other, the only tool I could find that had a pointed tip. I closed the door behind me and stepped out into the dark, starless night.

I swung the beam of light around to the back of the house and saw the creature. A porcupine. I almost laughed. Even somebody from the city knows that porcupines are not dangerous as long as you don't step on them. It was sitting on a pile of scrap wood and gnawing on the unpainted siding of the house.

"Go away, you!" I shouted.

Porcupines make up in tenacity what they lack in speed of response. The bristles stood up on end, but otherwise the dumb creature just looked at me. I got a little closer and banged on the edge of the woodpile with my log roller. It backed up an inch, and I was encouraged. I banged harder, and the porcupine stepped down from the woodpile.

I was not sure how fast a porcupine could move, so I rushed back inside.

"What was it?" Snaige asked.

"Porcupine," I said and laughed derisively. "I scared him off."

I had my clothes off and just slipped under the sheets

when the gnawing sounded again. It felt as if my brother had built an echo chamber instead of a house.

"Get the job done right this time," Snaige said. She was turning into a pioneer-type woman — straightforward. No nonsense. This time I went out in just my jeans, figuring that the upper part of my body was safe from an animal only a foot and a half tall.

I was still not eager to touch the porcupine with a stick, so I picked up some firewood and started to throw pieces at it. The porcupine stared at me with the same dumb eyes until I nicked it with a piece of wood, and it lumbered down off its perch.

"Ha!" I said and went back in and got undressed.

Country women value their sleep. It gives them strength for chopping wood during the day. When the gnawing started again, I lay silently on my side of the vinyl bed. Finally, Snaige threw back the covers.

"Never send a boy to do a man's job," she said enigmatically, then told me to hold the flashlight. She slipped on a pair of gumboots and took a shovel, and then led the way outside. Black gumboots and a frilly cotton nightgown looked attractive under the circumstance, but I thought I'd better keep my mouth shut.

The porcupine bristled in the beam of my flashlight. I had to admire it by this point. After all, we'd met twice before, and we were almost friends. Snaige raised the shovel over her shoulder and gave the porcupine a mighty blow on its head with the flat part of her weapon. It fell onto the earth and lay inert. The porcupine was dead, I was sure, and this seemed like a terribly disproportionate form of revenge. Terrible and magnificent at the same time.

"It's deceased," I said.

"We'll bury it in the morning. Now let's go get some sleep."

I lay awake on the vinyl bed for a long time after my wife's breathing became regular with sleep. I wondered if I should feel diminished by the night's events, but decided against it. My wife had merely risen in stature while I remained the same.

The porcupine did not come back that night, and the next day it was gone from the place where it had fallen. It never returned to disturb our slumber after that. The porcupine had learned its lesson. As for me, I was still learning mine.

※

Snaige seemed to have access through relatives to a lot of rustic places. She described them with great lyricism involving moonlight through pines, sunsets over water, wolves howling in the distance, and silent canoes from which the rich shoreline flora and fauna could be observed. And so it was that I found myself in a canoe piled high with sleeping bags and food, paddling gingerly a mile down the wide, slow river to a cottage deep in the forest. After two years in Paris, I had forgotten how close the wilderness was in Canada. As we unpacked the canoe, a great blue heron swept over us, and when we carried our belongings up to the cottage, I was instructed to use my paddle to thump the earth to warn off rattlesnakes.

Her uncle had delighted in warning us about the rattlesnakes. We were always to wear rubber boots, and if we did come across a rattlesnake and killed it, we were to separate the two parts we had cut in half because legend said they could rejoin at night. This was a ridiculous proposition, but what seemed ridiculous in the city became plausible in the wilderness. Even at midday, the cottage lay in the dim green light of the pine forest, and there were only oil lamps for light and a propane stove for cooking. We hauled water up from the river in buckets.

I wasn't exactly uneasy, but I was wary.

We took the canoe out for a paddle down the river with the odd cottage here and there, but mostly vast expanses of crown land nearby. I learned the J-stroke. As we paddled, we passed a swimming beaver that dove with a slap of the tail if we drew too close, and thin water snakes with their heads raised like periscopes above the water. A water snake is an alarming creature at first, but they don't bite and they are somewhat elegant. I was beginning to come around.

After a quick dinner, we took the canoe back out in the evening, portaged to a nearby lake, and started to fish just as a full moon came up. It became one of those nights when the moon was so bright, we cast shadows on the water. Soon, distant wolves began to howl at the moon, and the strangeness of the sound was both appealing and a little frightening.

The next day I took the canoe out on my own, and as I watched the surface of the river, I saw something moving along in the distance. It was an odd shape, symmetrical. As I paddled over, I saw it was a fishing bobber, which moved with the current, and then against it, and finally across it. Even a greenhorn like me could figure out there was a fish on the other end of the line. I paddled over and plunged my hand under the bobber, turned the line a couple of times around my hand, and pulled up. If the line hadn't been wrapped around my hand, I would have dropped it, because I pulled up a two-foot pike with exquisitely sharp teeth and a three-pronged hook the size of a gaff sticking out of its mouth.

I tossed the fish into the front of the canoe. Luckily, it was tired and didn't flop around too much. Thus I went from being a Parisian boulevardier to the hunter returning to his woman with his catch. Something about the rocky Canadian Shield brought out the Canadian in me. I would gut and clean the fish, and then go for a beer while my wife cooked it.

Actually, we didn't have any beer. In a place without ice, it made no sense to have beer, so we only had red wine. Snaige was not a big cook at the time. I would cook the fish.

I was finishing up the ghastly job of filleting the fish on a rock by the shore when I heard the put-put of a small outboard from across the way. Over came a geezer in an old wooden boat. He was dressed in a woolen checked jacket and had a hat with a pronounced bill and earflaps turned up. I looked up from the rock where I was mired in guts. He cut his motor just offshore.

"You left a lot of meat on the bones," he said.

This was my introduction to the neighbour, Tony. It was also my introduction to outdoorsmen, who have opinions.

"I'm a little out of practice," I said.

"Found the fish in the river, did you?"

It seemed a dumb question, so I just nodded.

"I think I recognize the bobber."

It was a red and white bobber, the kind sold in Canadian Tire stores across the country. It was hard to imagine any-one recognizing one as his own, but I could see where he was going with this.

"Did you lose a fish?" I asked.

"It broke the line off the pole I had sticking out from the shore."

"Untended line, was it?" I asked. It was illegal to fish with an untended line. Tony said nothing. He took my point. In the silence, though, I was suddenly overcome with magnanimity.

"You want the fish?" I asked.

"No. You brought the fish in. The fish is yours. I want the hook, sinker, and bobber."

So this was how wilderness justice played out. It seemed a fair deal. What he wanted cost under a dollar.

We made the trade and then, having done business, we set to talking. He warned me not to leave food behind in the cabin after we left. He told me about a bear that had gone through the wall of a hunting lodge when the hunters left their food behind them.

"Through the wall?" I asked incredulously.

"I guess it couldn't find the door," Tony said.

It's always fun to alarm the greenhorns.

"Have you been to the falls at the end of the river?" Tony asked. "It's pretty impressive down there. The water shoots down in three cataracts, and if you portage around it, you can paddle all the way to Georgian Bay. And there's some good fishing along the way."

"Are the falls very far?" I asked.

"About five miles. The portage around the falls is long, but it's worth it."

"I think I could handle paddling five miles," I said, "but I don't know about the portage. I don't think I could make it."

"A young man like you?"

"I'm a bit out of shape."

"You don't have to be strong to carry a canoe. The trick is all in the balance. You take the thwart in two hands and lift the canoe onto your shoulders in one smooth sweep. Then you find the centre and the canoe almost carries itself. It's not much harder than riding a bike."

I was still doubtful.

"This canoe must weigh sixty pounds," I said.

"The weight is beside the point. You take a sixty-six-pound bag of Portland cement, and you'd be lucky to carry it a hundred yards. That calls for brute strength. But a canoe is big and long and the weight is all spread out. You'd be surprised how much you can carry if you go about it the right way. Once you find the balance point, there's no stopping you from going any distance you want."

We talked for a while longer. I found out he was almost eighty years old, getting on a bit in age for a remote place like the one he lived in. When he returned to his property, I watched him from the distance and saw him hang on to a rope instead of a bannister to help pull himself up the hill to his cottage. There was a geezer nearing the end of his stay in the wilderness. As it turned out, a younger geezer was about to start his.

In retrospect, I came to realize he was fishing for a buyer. I came to wonder if Snaige had made some kind of a pact with him. When his cottage came up for sale at the end of the season, it was priced ridiculously low. Even an unemployed aspiring writer could afford it, with a little help from his in-laws.

※

Tony was an outrageous storyteller, but for once, the eighty-five-year-old shyster who had sold me my cottage was not lying. He called me out of the blue years after I'd last spoken to him.

"Take me out there one last time before I die, and I'll show you this hidden lake where the bass are so thick and hungry, they snap at each other's tails."

I'd owned his place for five years, and he was far too old to go out, but the call of the wild was still in him.

The hidden lake was a hard place to get to. We bushwhacked for two hours through dense undergrowth and paddled out in a canoe so full of leaks that I needed a bailer the size of a stock pot. But he was right about the fishing. The bass were so thick, I could see them cruising like schools of sunfish under the canoe. We caught our limit so fast we could have eaten our shore lunch before nine a.m.

I took one last look at the small lake, offered my aged guide my arm to hold on to, slung the backpack full of fish onto my shoulders, and tried to memorize the landmarks on our way out so that I would know how to get in there the next time I came.

The story was too good to keep quiet about, and the first person I told was a friend who also happens to be my dentist.

"Where did you say this lake was?"

"Oh, downstream from my cottage."

That covered more than a hundred square miles of bush dense with mosquitoes.

"Which side?"

"The one with the swamp."

That lowered the square mileage to about ninety-five.

It may have been my imagination, but my friend the dentist seemed to wield his drill with a little less than the usual skill after that.

I could not resist telling it at our next cottagers' meeting either. There were only nine cottages on our river, so we all fit snugly into one screened porch. After I told the story, silence fell on the normally vivacious group, until my neighbour Ken asked the same question that my dentist had.

"Downriver," I said.

As upriver meant only half a mile, and downriver meant over ten, I had not narrowed down the field very much.

"Could you be a bit more specific?"

"You know, the bush was so dense, I'm not even sure I could find the way again."

Ken looked at me with a mixture of hurt and irritation. "You can trust me," the look seemed to say. "I'm your neighbour." If only he knew how hard it was to keep from blurting out the secret.

By then we had two young boys, so I was accustomed to my words having absolutely no effect on anyone's behaviour. If only my kids listened to what I said the same way my neighbours did. My story about the secret fishing hole had set off a mini-version of a gold rush.

The first inkling came in the lumberyard in Mactier.

"Are you on the Gibson River?" the clerk asked.

"Yep," I answered in my best version of Muskoka terse.

"Know anything about this bass lake around there?"

"Just rumours. Why?"

"This fellow named Ken told us about some lake in there where the bass are so hungry they snap at each other's tails.

Me and a few of the boys from the hunt camp are going to get together a crew on ATVs and go looking for it. Directions might save us a little time."

My mood was dark as I boated down the river to my cottage. If Ken could spill the beans to a whole town, then what were the other cottagers doing? I could imagine them poring over topographical maps in the cottages on either side of me.

Was it my imagination, or did a kind of surveillance start on me? Every time I headed downriver with a fishing rod, one of my neighbours seemed to head out a few minutes later.

My dentist and his friend came canoe camping on our river. His friend told me that the dentist had spent a day bushwhacking with a compass, a topographical map, and a fishing rod. He had been lost in the bush for a day, and the only lake he found did not have any fish in it. After that time, my dentist kept steering me toward the bar whenever we met at a party.

I noticed another one of my neighbours, a young man named Peter, heading down the river with a mountain bike in his boat. I waved at him, but he didn't seem to notice me. It was only weeks later that his father told me he had been riding the old logging trails, looking for a lake where the bass were so hungry they snapped at each other's tails.

I learned my lesson. I hung up my fishing rod and went to ground for a year. I told my neighbours I had given up fishing. I bought a pair of binoculars and checked to see if my neighbours had their fish chains in the water when they returned from downriver. If they did, I watched them until they landed to see if their stringers were full of bass. None were.

Two years later, I figured the heat was down, so I took

Snaige and my two young boys to my secret fishing hole. I was worried that the place might have been cleaned out by the ATV gangs that had gone out to look for my secret, but when my son and I took the leaky canoe out, I could see the bass in schools under the boat. We caught our limit in an hour.

I thought that all had turned out well enough in the end, but I noticed that my older son was watching the landmarks on the way back out. "This place is incredible," he said. "Wait until I tell the neighbours about it."

※

Like most people who live in cities, I pretty well lost a keen sense of nature's cycles. Of course, one cannot live in Canada and be utterly unaware of the changing seasons. I knew winter had arrived when the windshield wiper fluid I used went from pink to blue and I had to root through the garbage in my car trunk for the window scraper. But for the most part, nature was what happened outside the window of the climate-controlled building where I worked.

Except at the cottage.

I couldn't actually get to the cottage in winter because our river froze imperfectly so I couldn't go in by boat or on foot, but I compensated by dreaming about it. When I stared out the window at work, I imagined the cottage like some kind of Ontario version of a Dickensian Christmas scene. I pictured the cabin with fat snowflakes falling over it. Then I couldn't remember if I had turned off the propane when we closed up for the fall. I imagined the pilot lights on the stove blowing out, and the cabin filling with poisonous gas.

The first person I thought of for help was my cottage neighbour Keith. He was retired and had taught me all about propane and a hundred other skills that were useful in the wilderness. He was a good friend at the cottage, but we did not see much of each other in the city. Keith would know what to do about leaking gas, but it would have been silly to call him for advice about a place I couldn't get to.

In late April, Snaige and my sons joined me in the motorboat as soon as there was a channel through the ice. Wet mounds of snow still lay in the shadows on the shoreline, and we left muddy tracks as we walked through the old drifts. The light through the bare trees was clear and sharp and my son picked some wintergreen to make tea. Hardly any wildlife was stirring yet, and the only sound was the ice on the water creaking and groaning when the wind shifted and moved the channel of open water, or closed it completely until the next gust. The propane tank in the cabin was safely off. For the first few hours until the wood stove heated up, we stamped our feet while clearing out mouse nests that had accumulated over the winter.

Since Keith was retired, I often found him up at the cottage when I arrived, but this time he was nowhere to be seen. His cottage stood shuttered and closed up tight.

Nobody went up to the cottage in May when the black flies were thick. It was a time when nature showed its perversity because the pike fishing was best when none of us could get at them.

I found out in May that my neighbour Keith had had a stroke over the winter. One of the other neighbours called to tell me. I was a bit nervous about phoning him in case his speech was badly impaired, but he sounded pretty good when I had him on the line. His interest picked up when he found I was planning to build a guest cabin at my place, and he gave me a few tips about how to set the wooden posts on the rocks. On the Gibson River all of us had to become experts in the arcane arts of the self-reliant: water pump maintenance, carpentry, and tree felling.

By June, the bass were jumping all over, something they only did until bass season opened. The great blue heron had established their territories, and the trees still looked bright green in their new leaves. The woods were alive with the sounds of invisible animals and I still managed to get spooked on my way to the outhouse at night when the chipmunks running through the undergrowth sounded like a bear in full charge. My boys made their first leaps off the dock into the river, but they came out blue and shivering before jumping again.

One day during that weekend in early June, we heard Keith's outboard on the river and the kids went running down to his dock to meet him; his wife, Emma; and their small black dog who always greeted us as if we were part of the family. Emma had a round, smiling face and the kids treated her as a stand-in grandmother at the cottage. Keith's face was rugged and proudly worn, the way a man in his seventies should look. We helped carry the bags up to his cottage because in addition to the stroke, his arthritis was bothering him, so he wore a brace on his knee and he had a hard time taking the hill. When he had rested up a bit, he came over to check out my new guest cabin. I pointed out the mistakes I had made, but he calmed me down about them.

"Carpentry is not an exact science," he said, shifting his weight off his bad knee. He was letting me know that a man did the best he could and then lived with the results. There was no use worrying about something you couldn't change.

Gibson River country was pretty remote for cottages, and we liked it that way. Still, it could be lonely up there sometimes, and it was pleasant to look out that night and see the light spilling out of Keith and Emma's windows.

I was raking our yard the next day when Emma came over carrying her big Coleman water jug. Drinking water was precious at our cottages because there were too many rocks and swamps for decent wells, and the river water was black with dissolved minerals.

"I brought you some water if you want it," Emma said.

"Going home already?"

"We'd planned to stay a week, but Keith isn't feeling well." She leaned up against our high deck, and for the first time I could remember, she looked tired. It wasn't easy taking care of a man with bad knees who had had a stroke. "To tell you the truth," she said, "I think our days up here are finished."

The kids were off on a hike with my wife, so I went down alone to my neighbours' dock to say goodbye to Keith. He was in pain, I guess, and he kept looking back up at the cottage the way I always did when I was ready to leave, making sure he hadn't forgotten anything and the house was closed properly.

By July, our new guest cabin was furnished with creaky old beds from the city, and we were ready for visitors. Kids were jumping off the dock and building tree houses as the adults barbecued ribs and drank far too many gin and tonics. I managed to take apart an old Johnson outboard, but couldn't get it back together again. By August, the mosquitoes were not too bad and hundreds of cobalt-blue dragonflies played mating games over the water. We watched processions of summer-camp canoeists head down our river toward Georgian Bay, and our own nine-year-old made his first long paddle down the river with a friend as I watched anxiously from our dock with binoculars, ready to go out in the motorboat if they needed help.

But ours was the only active cottage of the four on the north side of the river. One neighbour was a widow who never came up anymore, and there was no further sign of Keith and Emma. Even the Renners' cottage, which normally held two generations each weekend, lay quiet all summer long.

One Friday afternoon in early October, I called up Keith and Emma to find out if Keith was doing any better. When I got no answer at their home, I called their son Rob, a man around my own age. He told me Keith had died of a stroke two days earlier and he invited me to the memorial service.

Up at the Gibson River that October weekend, I could feel the bite in the air and it was time to start thinking about pulling the floating dock out of the river and putting it up on its winter blocks. Some of the leaves had yellowed early, and soon the river would be a dark ribbon between two hills flaming with colour.

We walked over to Keith's cottage to make sure it was closed up tight, because neither Emma nor their son Rob might have time to do a proper closing before winter. The river seemed lonely that weekend. There would be a couple more trips up to the cottage but the swimming was done and there was not much scrambling of wildlife through the bush.

Only a lone great blue heron still winged over the water like some kind of final sentinel.

Out on the dock that night, I felt the bittersweet feeling that always came over me at the end of another season. It would be sad to close up, but at least I would have the spring opening to look forward to.

⊠

Time moved slowly on the Gibson River, but it moved nevertheless in its unstoppable way. We saw generations come and go over twenty-five years there.

I used to go up the hill to our place with a propane tank in each hand, huffing and puffing, but doing it anyway. In more recent years, I had managed only one tank at a time, and then, after I threw out my back, Snaige would take one side of the handle and I the other before going up.

Finally, Snaige broke her leg one spring and there was no question of her going up that season. The more we thought about it, the more it seemed like there would be no going up there in any season at all. I remembered old Tony who had sold us the place. He used to pull himself up the hill using a rope tied to trees as a handrail until he could pull himself up no more. Our neighbour Keith had had to give the place up too. The boys who had grown up catching frogs down by the river and alerting us to the occasional rattlesnake had now moved away, and it looked like they would never be going up there anymore, not much anyway.

So it was time for us to sell.

Literary types abhor sentimentality. It's used too often to

market products to us, but it is hard to let things go. Even though we have left behind the cottage now and will never go back, our children will be forever jumping off the high cliff that gave us so much anxiety; the hummingbirds will still swoop and fight at the feeder outside the screened porch; and the water will continue to lap in its mesmerizing way down on the river, seeming to express infinity.

It's a place for others to find now, and if they do, they might also find that secret lake where the bass are so thick, they snap at each other's tails.

AFTER *the* PARTY

I stared down into the bright light of the classroom overhead projector and moved my pencil to point at the picture on the acetate sheet.

"It is a glass!" I said loudly and clearly.

The class responded with a sound they might make if they were at the dentist's and their mouths were full of instruments: "*I i a gla.*"

I elaborated, "It is a glass of wine." I used my best bright tone, upbeat and mildly delighted. As if after head trauma I had thought long and hard about what the item might be and had finally discovered the right word for it.

Again like dental patients, my students responded from the darkness of the classroom, "*I i a gla uh why.*"

This was an adult beginners' language class at Humber College. Those among them who studied hard for the next twenty-four weeks would end up with enough basic vocabulary to understand some English. They in turn would never be understood by anyone but me. Vietnamese words did not end with consonants and no amount of chorus repetition could make them sound out the consonant at the end of an English word.

I pointed to another image.

"Here is a bottle of bourbon." If I had expressed mild delight at the glass of wine, I expressed something bordering on jubilation for the bourbon.

"He i a bouh uh boobah."

It was 1982 and Canada had taken in the Vietnamese Boat People, as they were called at the time. They had suffered terribly and Canada was trying to do the right thing by them, to equip them for life in a new land. They received winter coats, sixty dollars a week, and twenty-four weeks of English lessons before being let loose in the land of doughnuts and toboggans.

The bright light blinded me as I stared into the projector. I should have been using a pointer and standing at the screen at the front of the class, but there was no pointer. I improvised, working my way through jars of wine, cups of whisky, bowls of vodka, tumblers of tequila, spoons of beer, jugs of brandy, and so on. To vary the lesson, I occasionally changed the containers to boxes and packages, both of which contained cigarettes. I worked in lighters wherever I could.

"You're a terrible person," Janice would say. She sat in the vast staff room at a desk across from mine, a jaunty scarf around her middle-aged neck. Three of the most recent gifts of porcelain statues she had received from students stood on the bookcase behind her.

Vietnamese students had a habit of buying their teachers gifts, and since we changed classes every six weeks, we received gifts every six weeks. Porcelain statues were very popular, as were plaques, sashes for the women, and scarves for the men.

I had no need of those things. None of us needed those things, but they were the heartfelt expressions of gratitude of men and women who had risked imprisonment, death at sea, and disease in crowded refugee camps. I was touched by their gratitude, but I wanted their good intentions to hit the mark. The students knew me well, and I received only gifts of liquor, cigarettes, and lighters.

I was staring into the intense overhead projector lamp when the classroom door banged open and someone flipped the classroom light switch on.

"If I told you once, I told you twice! No eating in the classroom!"

It was Gerry the janitor, the scourge of the campus. He had a bum leg that people said came from an injury in the army thirty years ago in Korea. Thus he was morally superior to us, and we were all afraid of him. And he knew it. He terrorized students, teachers, and administrators alike. He was righteous in his cleanliness and ready to smite anyone who wasn't.

I was blinded from staring at the overhead projector and Gerry was hard to make out clearly. For a moment, there seemed to be two of him — double Gerry, double trouble.

"There's going to be a party in this room later today," I said to him. "There's going to be food here anyway."

Gerry didn't argue. Like God, he did not enter into negotiations — he proclaimed and left it at that. Gerry slammed the door, and I turned to placate the class. They were not all Vietnamese. A few were Poles who were part of the immigrant wave after Solidarity, the democracy movement, that was closed down in Warsaw, and a couple were Latin Americans fleeing murderous dictators. The Latins were leftists, and the Poles and Vietnamese despised them for their politics. But the Vietnamese and the Poles, although they shared politics, shared practically nothing else. Canada was supposed to be the land of two solitudes, but in my classroom I had at least three.

How to explain Gerry to a room full of mixed new Canadians without the language? I shrugged at them and smiled. Sometimes gestures were worth more than language. I looked at my watch. We had five more minutes to go in the class, but I decided we all needed a break. I threw open the door and led the way out.

The dominant cultures behaved differently in the halls. The Vietnamese men squatted against the walls, smoking. The Latins stood in groups and talked to one another while the Poles made for the cafeteria with massive thermoses of tea or coffee and sacks of buns, sandwiches, cakes, and those long, thin hunter's sausages, which I occasionally got offered as I passed by. I'd snap off six inches to tide me over between classes.

I stepped into the bathroom to find my colleague, Maurice, washing his hair in the sink, having stoppered the drain with a knot of wet toilet paper.

"Can you give me a hand?" he asked. He had a pencil moustache and dark blond hair ordinarily combed in a style that could only be called "dashing." He worked out, and it showed. He was looking up from the sink with soap running toward his eye.

"Sure," I said

He turned his face back down. I cupped my hands and sloshed water over his head.

"I could use a scalp massage," said Maurice.

"Fuck off."

Maurice was gay, as were all the other male teachers of the faculty except Declan and me. We were outnumbered five to two, and the gay guys were always lobbying us to join their high-spirited team. Maurice had been christened "Morris" by his Irish parents, but he had a certain Noël Coward style he liked to project. He lived in a loft in the old garment district when it was still illegal to do that. He didn't have his own bathroom and his bed was a fold-out couch in case a city inspector came by. He could also be confrontational. One morning I took a call from him when he was arrested on a streetcar for getting into an argument with the driver when he was five cents short on the fare.

"Pass me some paper towels," he said when I'd finished rinsing.

"Trying to make a good impression?" I asked.

"We have a graduation party later today. I want to look my best."

We had a vast number of classes with irregular intakes as well as one-off additions of students who were placed at whatever level seemed right for them. We were like a third world bus station, and every couple of weeks we declared a graduation as thirty or twice that number departed on their voyage into life. The students brought their own national food to the graduation party, we laid out ashtrays in the class, and sometimes we even put on our own play for the students.

I stepped into the staff room where Margitta was laying out copies of a script, a reading from Dylan Thomas's *A Child's Christmas in Wales*. It would do no good to argue with Margitta that the grads would understand nothing of this lyrical hymn to Welsh childhood, nor to add that we were in June and nothing was worse than a Christmas reading outside the season. Margitta aimed high. A nervous, brilliant, and excitable teacher, Margitta was remarkable for the way she coordinated her outfits. The bow in her hair matched her dress, her bag, and her shoes, and once when I accidentally stepped into the dressing room where she was changing for a school play, I saw that her underwear matched her overwear too. She had been born in East Prussia and was carried out as a baby in her parents' arms when the Soviets deported all the Germans after the war. Somehow, this childhood trauma had resulted in extreme fashion sense.

The federal agency that provided the stream of students to our school would decide on a Thursday that it needed classes for another two hundred new immigrants on the following Monday, and Humber College never refused an offer of new bums in seats. Calls went out for teachers at a time when second-language training was not that common, so teachers were mostly untrained people who were at loose ends, ready at the drop of a hat to pick up a few days, weeks, or months of work. I was one of them, recently back from my Bohemian years in Paris and now out of work.

Bill Newman was a white man who spoke like a black man because he had been raised in Guyana. He had a fine voice and occasionally led singalongs when there were no parties to ease Friday afternoons into the weekend. Jane was a Russian who had immigrated to Canada, and aside from Janice and Declan, the rest were a grab bag of oddballs, neurotics, and people passing through on the way to somewhere else. This was not our real life. We all had different destinations in mind, but we were thrown together at this bus terminal of a school until we moved on.

The campus was an old warehouse on Industry Street in

a depressed area near Mount Dennis, a neighbourhood that would go on to be rated by *Toronto Life* magazine as the least desirable neighbourhood in all of Toronto. Across the street was a wide, low building belonging to Moore Business Forms, and up the street was the Kodak film processing plant. Behind us were dozens of small warehouses and workshops, and scattered among these, lone frame houses with chain-links fences and dogs barking in the yards.

If we were lucky, a Friday at our campus was all about the party. Earnest graduating students came bearing trays of spring rolls, sliced smoked sausages, and a vast variety of meat-in-pastry that seemed to exist in different forms in every culture. Men brought drinks. Clothing varied from traditional sashes and dresses for some women to low-cut gowns and stilettos worn by the dressier Polish women. The impact was jarring, like a low-rent nightclub colliding with a multicultural dance festival.

Presiding over the speeches at the front of our biggest classroom was Two-Cup Shea, the chairman of the campus, the highest administrator in our refurbished warehouse. He was a man of ambitions, this fiefdom one rung on his ladder to greater things. He had the smooth and chiselled face of a TV announcer and prematurely white hair combed into a bouffant. He did not speak so much as pronounce, and he used wide arm gestures that looked dramatic and heartfelt in front of a crowd but were alarming in a small space.

His signature trait was that he walked the halls with two takeout cups of coffee, one perched on top of the other, in one hand and a briefcase in the other hand. He was remarkably good at balancing these cups. The double-cup manoeuvre made him seem driven, talented, and ambitious. All of that might have impressed the higher powers but there were no higher powers at our satellite campus. Still, Two-Cup Shea was ready to make a good impression if they ever showed up.

Now Two-Cup stood before sixty students and nine of us teachers stood behind him, the chorus to his solo. Two-Cup liked to talk about public service, stressing how the new graduates should "give back" now that they had received the support of the state.

For the students, one journey was ending and another would begin after this, the last day of their studies. With spotty English, they would collect their last federal subsidy cheques and head off on Monday morning to the Manpower office, where engineers would be offered factory jobs, doctors offered aide positions in hospitals, and women offered a variety of cleaning jobs regardless of their degrees.

Two-Cup gave his speech and went off to a "meeting" right after his talk. He never ate with the students, being leery of foreign food. Everybody was eager to get out early on a Friday, but the Manpower office mandated classes run until three p.m. Once Two-Cup spoke and left, Margitta stepped forward and directed each of us to read our part from *A Child's Christmas in Wales*. As I expected, most student faces went blank, although a few of the more earnest students tried to look interested. Each of the ethnic groups sang a song, and all of the teachers looked appreciative and clapped enthusiastically at the end of the concert.

Among the three dominant ethnicities in the room, we also had a lone South Asian student. He stood out for not having any national compatriots in the school and for being tall, gangly, and goofy in a young man sort of way. He had adopted a "Canadian" name and called himself Jack, a name none of the Vietnamese would be able to pronounce. He wore a thin beard and a baseball cap, and he stood and recited a rather long poem in a language I did not recognize. It might have been English.

Once the formalities were over, the teachers were encouraged to descend first to the buffet placed on pushed-together school desks. There was not only wine on the table but many bottles of hard liquor as well. One of the Polish men poured me half a plastic glass of bison grass vodka.

"What do you mix this with, Marek?" I didn't know if his name was Marek, but there were a lot of Polish men named Marek. He might be one of them.

Marek had never heard the word "mix" before and didn't know what I meant.

"Cocktail?" I asked.

Marek laughed. Cocktails were for women. Men drank their vodka straight up. I took the glass with me and sat down beside a pair of graduating Vietnamese men, the good friends Duong Bac and Chi Lam. The former had a lively spark to him and could make funny faces, and the latter was his good-humoured sidekick.

I had been their first teacher, and they had been my first students twenty-four weeks earlier, when I had accepted the job just before Christmas in order to make some money to buy presents. Now it was half a year later and they were ready to move on. I felt sentimental about them, all the more so after I finished the half glass of vodka. The Polish men were relentlessly hospitable with the vodka, and I had to refill the glass with water from the fountain in the hall, or else it would be topped up until I toppled over. The women were relentlessly hospitable with food, and I knew I had to get out of the room soon or I'd be stuffed like meat in a sausage casing.

Most of the teachers had to go back to their afternoon classes, but the three homeroom teachers stayed behind, among them Declan, the Irish charmer, good with a joke, flexible and inventive around rules and regulations, passionate about sports, and appreciative of a pretty face. As the only other straight man in the department, he was part of my team.

"Stick around," he'd suggested when I said I had to go to another class. "Give your students some homework to do in their seats and come back to the party." I appreciated the gesture, but I had to get away from the hospitality or else call Snaige to drive me home after work. I said I'd be back for coffee in an hour.

When I did return, the mood in the room had shifted considerably. The ethnic celebration types had fled with their sashes and their earnest faces, and the partiers remained behind. The lights were mostly turned off. Someone had brought a record player, and while an hour earlier the tunes were mostly upbeat ABBA, now they were the slow songs from the Beatles. The room was full of cigarette smoke and the schoolroom romances were in full drunken splendour. The men draped themselves over the women and one of the men was rubbing the bare back of a Polish bombshell in a low-cut dress. Alone among the Europeans stood Jack by the bar, swaying slowly to the music, watching the dancers with admiring eyes, and holding in his hand a glass of vodka, obviously not his first.

Declan was the only teacher among them, sitting on a chair and smiling benignly at his dancing students. I poured myself a cup of coffee and sat down beside him for a moment.

"This is getting a little heavy," I said.

"What do you mean?"

"It's like high school with alcohol."

He looked at his watch. It was only two o'clock and there was another hour to go before the students would be released. "Let them bask in the glory of their final day," he said. "On Monday, it's going to be the factory floor if they're lucky and pounding the pavement if they're not. Look at them, young and in love and full of hope."

I thought he must be drunk. I had no more classes for the rest of the day, but I couldn't leave early. I wandered down to the office. It was June, a gloriously warm afternoon, and the office had no one left in it but a receptionist. Once Two-Cup took off early, the office manager let the support staff leave early too. We were just a skeleton crew, waiting out our time until the clock struck three. I went back to the staff room, just down the hall from where the party was happening, in order to file away the cards that recorded the student grades.

"Antanas."

My name was said very quietly, but there was something about the tone that troubled me. I looked down the hall and saw Declan standing at the classroom door where the party was taking place. Someone was trying to open it from the inside, but Declan was pulling hard to hold it shut.

"Help me," he said, again very quietly. I ran down to the end of the hall and held the doorknob with him as it was tugged from inside.

"What are we doing?" I asked.

"There's a ruckus inside. I don't want it to spill into the hall."

We looked at each other, uncertain.

"We're supposed to be the teachers," I said.

"I suppose we are," he said sadly.

Real teachers didn't try to hide a problem. They solved it. Some curious students from other classes were already watching us in the hall.

We pushed the door open and stepped inside, and immediately two Vietnamese women fled the room and Declan slammed the door behind them. On the floor lay Jack and on top of him sat a large Polish Marek who was slapping his face. Jack's head bounced from side to side as he took the slow, systematic blows. Around them stood a circle of men and women like kids watching a fight in the schoolyard. I grasped Marek by the shoulders and pulled him off. He staggered away.

As soon as Marek was off his chest, Jack leaped up and bounced on his toes like a boxer, holding fists up defensively and circling the ring of faces. Goofy as always, he looked ridiculous with his cow-licked hair and slack face. I reached forward and put my hand on his shoulder.

"No touch!" he shouted. He was very drunk and that probably saved him from getting hurt as Marek slapped him around. Jack was flexible, wobbly, his hat missing and his hair matted with sweat.

In American parlance, we had a "situation" in the room. I glanced at Declan at the door and we shared another insight. There were no figures of authority in the building. Just us.

Poor Jack had stood drinking at the bar and watching the men hug women and rub their bare backs. He had wanted to rub a woman's bare back too, but when he tried, she shrieked, and the other men had come to her rescue: drunken gentlemen saving drunken damsels from a drunken young man who didn't know how to make the right moves.

Jack looked ridiculous, but he was ready to fight, and the men in the circle around him were willing to take him on if he lunged at one of them.

"Jack," I said, and when he was slow to respond, I said his name again. He looked at me, but I wasn't sure he was seeing me clearly. "I won't touch you. But you can take my arm," I said, and I moved my arm slightly away from my side, staying as still as I could. Jack stepped forward and linked his arm with mine. I had him.

"Let's get some air," I said.

Declan held open the door.

"Get your car from the lot and meet me at the side of the building," I said to Declan as I passed. "We'll take him home."

And then we stepped out into the corridor where the students who had heard the noise were lining both sides of the hall. We walked like the king and queen of England, stately, Jack nodding to students left and right, wobbling slightly. Everyone in the hall knew something was wrong, but no one knew exactly what it was. How often did teacher and student stroll the halls like this?

Out of nowhere came Maurice, suddenly walking on the other side of Jack.

"Take my arm too?" he asked. Maurice had a nose for trouble. He was so often in it himself that he was perpetually at the ready. Jack acquiesced, and now he was walking arm in arm between two men who flanked him like honour guards. The halls seemed to fill as we promenaded toward the side door of the campus.

"Is there a plan?" Maurice asked genially, smiling at the students we passed.

"We'll go to the side door and Declan will bring a car. Then we'll take him home."

Maurice nodded, in the game. Neither of us knew what was going through Jack's head. I didn't know what country he had come from. I didn't know his religion. Was alcohol forbidden to him? Where did he live, and if he had parents, what would they say to us? None of this was clear. All we knew was we had to get him out of the building.

We exited successfully behind the cafeteria, where there were a few paved delivery spots on a low hill that dropped a few feet down to the road where Declan would bring his car.

"Let's sit down!" I said, as if we'd been on a walk in the park and needed a short rest. Jack seemed game for everything, so the three of us sat on the edge of the pavement with our legs in front of us on the grassy slope that dropped below. It was a beautiful early summer day, a Friday afternoon that showed much promise for the weekend. Snaige and I might drive up that evening to Wasaga Beach or maybe stay in the city and meet some friends on a patio for drinks. All we had to do was get through this.

We waited. It seemed like a long time. We did not try to talk to Jack, and he did not try to talk to us. We were outside the range of our ordinary lives, suspended and waiting.

"Where's Declan with the car?" asked Maurice.

I didn't know at the time, but I later found out he was trying to start the engine of his Grand Marquis. The engine refused to turn over and he flooded it. Thus we were stranded on the summer hillside, our reinforcement gone missing.

"I'll go inside and find him," I said. I stood to go back into the school, but Jack shot his hand out to seize me by the ankle and caught me off balance. I went down face-first onto the pavement. I tried to act calmly. To make no false moves. From the pavement, I asked Jack what he had in mind.

"Don't go!" he said. Now we were in some kind of abandonment narrative. I spoke in reassuring terms, telling Jack to stay with Maurice, that I would be back in a moment, and I extricated myself from his grasp, rose, dusted myself off, and started toward the cafeteria door.

I heard a yelp behind me and turned to see Jack had bolted. He ran down the short hill onto the road and was running toward Industry Street with Maurice in pursuit. Maurice was fast, but Jack had long legs and he was like a gazelle fleeing a predator. I was a few seconds behind them.

Industry Street was the most aptly named road in Toronto. As Jack reached the intersection and ran into the middle of it, he looked to the right to see a transport truck coming at him. He froze and stared at it as the driver hit the brakes and began to veer to the left, into the oncoming lane. It was going to be very close, and then Maurice came in from behind and push-tackled Jack, who went down onto the far sidewalk. He was out of danger from the truck but he had banged his head on the concrete. As for the transport, the driver had veered so far left that he went slightly over the curb and stopped with his front wheels on the grass in front of our warehouse school.

Oncoming cars and trucks were blocked, as were the ones behind the transport, which had straddled the width of the road.

I came around to where Maurice stood over Jack, and the two of us looked down at him. He had closed his eyes, as if napping, but his lids shot open and he stared at us angrily.

"You know who I am?" he asked.

"You're Jack," I said.

"No! I am Kali, the Destroyer." And having established his otherworldly credentials, he banged his head on the sidewalk, whether to demonstrate his invincibility or commit suicide, I was unsure. Again, Maurice was faster than me, and he fell to the sidewalk and took Jack into a firm headlock with Jack's head on Maurice's lap. There was blood coming from Jack's scalp, and he struggled briefly, then turned his face sideways and vomited onto Maurice's lap.

By now we were in the centre of a traffic jam. Word had shot through the campus and hundreds of students stood on the front lawn, watching us. The first vehicle beyond us was a dark green Bell Telephone van, and the door opened and the installer stepped out.

"Don't worry," he called. "I've radioed the police."

Everything was going to change now. The police and the ambulance would come. Awkward excuses would be given. We'd need to explain that a school-sponsored party had gotten out of hand because the temporary teachers were useless overseers.

And everything did change in our lives, but not exactly in the way we expected.

✖

Later in the day, when the ambulances and the police had left, the traffic jam had cleared, and the students were gone, Maurice, Declan, and I were sitting in the staff room with the other teachers, rehashing what had happened. I'd called Maurice the hero, and so he was, likely having saved Jack's life. Now Maurice sat in his glory, feet up on the desk in front of him, hair combed back carefully in a retro wave, his pencil moustache impeccable but his trousers all wet where he'd rinsed them off.

We were unsure what would happen on Monday. Luckily, everyone was gone for the weekend at the main campus when we called in the incident, so we had left a phone message. But Two-Cup would be back after the weekend and a whole process of investigation would begin. We were almost all temps, so we'd likely take the blame. We could be swept away. Some were full-time, but most of the crew of gay men and I were on monthly contracts. They knew one another better than I did, and so they were talking about friends with bars and restaurants where they could get temporary jobs if bad became worse on Monday.

Monday wasn't the problem. Miraculously, no one complained about anything, and an unreported incident did not exist if it wasn't filed on paper.

But in our relief, we barely paid any attention to Maurice's cough. Colds were going around and summer colds were the worst. By the end of the month I was laid off, but just for the summer because student numbers were down. I'd be back in September.

Maurice wasn't there when I returned. He was sick, people said, on leave. It was worrisome, but he had just turned thirty, so how bad could it be?

And then others got sick. Kevin, and Rob, and eventually Dale too.

The world was changing in unexpected ways.

We weren't allowed to smoke in the staff room anymore and considered it a great affront to our adult rights. Security guards were installed at the campuses. To my surprise, I was offered a full-time position and I was moved to another campus, now teaching freshman composition to second-generation Italians who owned good cars and lived with their parents. Little by little, I began to realize I might really be a teacher.

And one by one, the funerals came. Dale wept freely at Maurice's funeral. Kevin's was very quiet. When I arrived at the visitation, there was no one there except for two sisters I never knew existed. The pastor forgot Rob's name at his memorial service, and then Dale died too. All of them and more were swept away.

The one gay teacher who survived was Bill Newman, whom I haven't seen in decades but who can be found on YouTube as the Calypso Crooner. I can watch him singing his songs — still with a spark of impishness, still with a slightly wicked grin although, like the rest of us from those days, he has put on weight and it shows under his Hawaiian shirt as he moves around the stage. That grin is all that's left of the high spirits of our time in the warehouse school.

My Vietnamese students, Duong Bac and Chi Lam, went different ways. I heard a rumour that the former went on to get on the wrong side of the law, and the latter became a restaurant chef. As to Jack and the Vietnamese and Poles, they blended in here. The Mareks became Marks and moved to Mississauga, their past lives no more than lingering accents.

The college where I still teach has become a serious and respected place. Jobs are tight and anyone who gets hired is grateful for the work and hopes to snag one of the rare full-time positions. But the spark of those early days has gone away, gone away with Maurice and Kevin, and Dale and Rob. No one smokes and there are few parties. The bottle of brandy I bought for Friday afternoon drinks has sat unopened in my desk drawer for fifteen years. We have moved from vodka to cookies and tea.

The bus station has closed. We have all arrived at our destinations.

1987

THE TURN *of the* KNOB

When I got cold feet about spending the night alone in a haunted house, I knew the one person who would be willing to come along with me was Rudy McToots. He was waiting for me on the porch of his Toronto house wearing a baseball cap and jacket with a small backpack at his feet. The biggest axe I had ever seen was leaning up against the railing.

When I tapped the horn for him to come down, he picked up the backpack and the axe. I stepped out of the car.

"What's the axe for?" I asked.

"Haven't you ever seen any horror movies?"

"Not for years. My wife doesn't like them."

"People get trapped inside the house. You need to have a way to break out."

"Leave the axe at home."

"What for?"

"We'll have a few drinks tonight. The last thing I want is you walking around with three cocktails inside you and an axe on your shoulder."

"You're sure?"

I was sure, and Rudy was nothing if not easygoing.

151

I'd heard about the haunted house from Vinnie, a student counsellor at my workplace, Humber College. Vinnie was the kind of woman who looked you in the eye, gave you hugs, and laughed at your jokes. People unburdened themselves to her all the time. I had done it more than once, and that made it all the stranger when Vinnie unburdened herself to us for a change. She told the staff in the teachers' lunchroom about the uncanny weekend she had spent in a country lodge up on the Rideau Canal. Four couples had rented a big old lodge, but they had found the atmosphere creepy. So creepy that they had fled in the middle of the night.

"All of you?" I asked.

"All of us."

"What time?"

"About two in the morning."

Vinnie was a counsellor, for heaven's sakes. She was supposed to be levelheaded. She wore woolen sweaters. If Vinnie and four other couples had been terrified, there was good reason for it.

"What, exactly, made you so terrified?" I asked.

"There was an aura in that house."

"Could you see it?"

"No, but we could sense it. We felt as if the walls were closing in on us."

"Group psychosis?" I asked.

"Which one of us has the psychology degree?"

"Could you tell me where this place is?"

I sold the idea to *Ontario Living*, where editor Liz Primeau would use it as a location piece with the ghost story as the hook. But she had her reservations.

"What if nothing happens?" Liz asked.

"Don't worry. There will be a story in this."

"But something has to happen for there to be a story."

"Something will happen."

"Something better happen."

I didn't really expect anything to happen but on the other hand I was just slightly worried that something might happen. Not entirely worried, but I had seen enough ghost films before I married a horror-movie-averse wife. The slight bit of worry made me look for a companion instead of doing it alone. I offered Rudy fifty dollars for companionship for the night, plus expenses. Those consisted of the gas for my car, a package of hot dogs, and a mickey of brandy.

✖

The Rideau Canal was in summer tourist territory, green and rocky with plenty of rivers. The lodge owner in the ramshackle office looked like he'd just gotten up from a nap without patting down his hair. After I prodded him, he told me a capsule history of the place as he wrote out the receipt — he said it had been a farmhouse a hundred years ago, but fishermen kept knocking on the door asking for a room for the night. Eventually the farmhouse expanded, one room at a time, and became a lodge, but not many people used the lodge anymore, just the cottages out on the lakeside.

"Any accidents ever happen here?" I asked.

"Accidents?" He looked up at me, troubled.

"Well, over a hundred years there must have been all kinds of ups and downs," I said. I guessed that the lodge wouldn't want to be known as haunted, so I was trying to come at the subject sideways.

"Just fresh air, good fishing, and plenty of happy families passing through. The only stories here are good stories. And by the way, how is it that the two of you want to rent the big place?"

I backed off. I told the owner a group of guys would join us at dawn to go fishing.

He nodded out of politeness, not really buying my story, but he finished writing the receipt and pocketed the cash I'd laid on the desk. Then he went out, got in his pickup, and drove away.

Rudy and I were the only ones in the place, not just in the lodge itself where we were staying, but also among the small frame cottages in a half circle facing the lake. The place felt like an empty stage in a theatre that hadn't been used since Anton Chekhov passed away.

The vast sitting room had a pair of worn leather armchairs set in front of a big stone fireplace with mirrored panels on the sides of the mantle. Past this were an industrial kitchen and then a dining room that could seat fifty people, but it hadn't been used for a long time. A big old-fashioned perambulator was stored in one corner and cast iron pans were stacked in haphazard columns of five and six. Institutional-sized cans of fruit salad and mixed vegetables were lined up on the counter, the dust on them thick. Someone had dragged a finger across the top of one of the cans, but that had been a long time ago and new dust filled the streak.

It was late in the day and the sun streamed low through the windows, adding no cheer to the place. The room smelled bad, like a small animal had died in a drawer that no one ever opened.

Rudy seemed insensitive to the gloomy atmosphere. He was like an eager spelunker, curious and optimistic, a male Pollyanna. We went down to the basement, which was vast, and found it compartmented by strange brick walls that reached almost to the ceiling. I boosted Rudy up and he shone a flashlight into the gap to see that these were big cisterns that had caught rainwater in earlier times. Animals had indeed fallen in there and found no way out. There seemed to be layers of rodents from the recently dead to the long-since expired.

"At least they're not running around upstairs," said Rudy.

There were three staircases in various additions, some of which had separate basements beneath them and some of which had only second storeys. The place had grown haphazardly, as if a room or a storey were added whenever a larger group wanted to come up. We took our bags up the steep, narrow main staircase and chose a bedroom with two single beds across from one another under a sloping ceiling.

By now, night was starting to fall, and I lit up the gas stove in the kitchen, found a pot that looked reasonably clean, and boiled up the hot dogs that we ate on buns with brandy and ginger ale on the side.

Then we waited. I kept topping up the drinks. First we were a little intimidated by the darkness outside, and then we became slightly bored. We began to take small excursions on our own. I'd go upstairs to our room to get another package of cigarettes from my bag, or Rudy would remember he had forgotten to look in the cold room in the kitchen. I half-hoped Rudy would disappear or become entangled in an adventure.

"I'm sorry I didn't bring my guitar," Rudy said at one point, and I was irritated with him for it. A guitar in a haunted house? It wasn't appropriate. We needed an atmosphere of dread and a climax of some kind. I began to wonder what Liz Primeau would say back at the magazine if nothing did happen. Yet as it got later and the room cooled when the mist came in off the lake, part of me hoped that nothing would happen.

We seated ourselves in front of the empty fireplace, I with the door to the corridor leading out of the house to my left, and Rudy to my right in another armchair with a bank of windows behind him. We had started to talk less and settled into silence while we stared at the fireplace. As I did, I noticed there was something strange about it. One of the two tall mirrors on either side of the mantle seemed to be askew somehow. I stood up and walked over to it.

The mirror was actually a cabinet door and as I opened it stacks of old photos and documents spilled onto the mantle and down onto the floor. The light from the overhead was poor, but I could see that these were old family photos. In some of the pictures, women had parasols and long white dresses. Men sat smiling in racing sculls.

"Why would anyone keep family photos in a place they rented out?" I asked Rudy.

"Maybe they had no place else to put them."

It was a moronic answer. Upbeat, yes, but not part of what the atmosphere should be.

"Tell you what," he said. "If there's anything remotely

haunted here, it wants to be encouraged. We need more atmosphere. Let's turn out all the lights and rely on candles."

We did that. We lit two candles and placed one on each end of the mantelpiece.

By now it was well after midnight. We sat in those arm-chairs, looking into the empty fireplace, and didn't talk very much. When I had to go to the bathroom, I took a candle with me.

"Do you think anything will happen?" Rudy asked when I returned.

"Something better happen."

"Maybe it already has."

"What's that supposed to mean?"

"Maybe more time has passed outside than in here. Maybe we're going to be nothing more than old photographs that some other generation is going to find when it opens the cup-board and the pictures fall out."

By two in the morning, we were tired and had stopped drinking and the alcohol was wearing off.

"I'm cold," said Rudy.

There was firewood piled up at the side of the fireplace, but no kindling. I walked around the kitchen with the candle in my hand and found some old paper towel rolls and cardboard boxes. I brought them back in, pulled apart the rolls to make them thinner and rolled some of the others to make them thicker to burn longer. The pieces of wood were pretty big, though, so it was going to be hard to get them going. I stacked everything as carefully as I could and then set three pieces of the smallest firewood I could find into a teepee. I lit a match to the bottom and then stood back. The finer paper flared up and the thicker cardboard caught, but it wasn't hot enough or long enough to make the firewood catch.

I scrounged some more and started again, and this time the wood did catch, but feebly. It must have been damp and the draw was poor and smoke started to come into the room. I went over behind Rudy and struggled with one of the windows, and I finally got it up.

Some of the smoke cleared out of the room, although a haze of it lingered up high near the ceiling. The pieces of firewood struggled to burn, always on the verge of going out, sometimes dying down, and sometimes bursting into flame.

We sat, and we waited. The pitiful fire didn't throw off much heat and the room grew colder.

Just then Rudy turned to speak to me, but before any words came out, I saw the window behind him slip in its casing and slam down onto the sill. The noise was deafening, like a gunshot.

The look on Rudy's face went from conversational to terrified, so much so that it seemed practically funny to me. Yet I was wound up and the noise was alarming and Rudy's terror was transferred to me.

We both ran in horror to the front door to get outside. I grasped the knob to turn it, and it came off in my hand. We were trapped inside.

"The axe!" said Rudy in despair.

We stood and listened. We could hear scratching coming from under the floorboards. We desperately hoped that nothing more would happen.

1988
A STORY to DIE FOR

In the stale chaos of her California bungalow, Rosalind Paquette could have auditioned for the role of Miss Havisham.

"Do you want a cup of tea?" she asked once she had shoved aside the mass of dirty dishes in the sink and added water to a chipped vase for the carnations I'd brought her.

"Sure."

"She's unusual," one of the Tillson clan back in Ontario had said and left it at that. Ted Allan, Norman Bethune's biographer, had been more direct. "She's crazy. I tried to write a biography of Tillson Lever Harrison but she wouldn't talk to me half the time, and she yelled at me the other half. Find another subject. Tillson Lever Harrison's story has broken the heart of more than one writer."

But I wanted to write the biography of Dr. Tillson Lever Harrison, the second-most famous Canadian in China. Harrison had been like Vronsky in *Anna Karenina* — dashing, charming, and disreputable. He'd helped the communists near the end of his life but decades earlier he'd abandoned poor Rosalind at the age of two when he joined Pancho Villa's revolution in Mexico. He also adventured his way through France in World War I, the Irish uprising, the

Chinese civil war, and many, many more places.

He'd charmed me posthumously. Not only did I want to write his biography, I needed to write his biography. Nobody was buying my novels. Maybe somebody would buy this story. But sources were scarce until I found out his daughter lived in Newport Beach. She was my last chance.

There were dirty teacups on the glass tabletop as well as saucers covered in crumbs and bits of crust from the toasts of yesteryear. The counter was stacked with dishes too. I saw streaks on the walls, which meant that the room had not been repainted in decades and when the work was done the first time, it had been before the invention of the paint roller.

Rosalind turned to ask me if I would like sugar in my tea. She was wearing a ruffled white shirt under her suit jacket, a puffy kind of shirt that a pirate or cavalier might put on. And she had spilled about half a cup of coffee on it some time in the past, leaving a great stain the size of a man's open hand. Who would wear such a thing to meet a stranger for the first time?

It was still morning but the house was airless and hot. What I would have liked was to get out of there. The place smelled bad and looked bad. But I calmed myself down. She was just an old lady and, besides, she acted nice enough. I reminded myself that I was after a book and a little stink and a messy house shouldn't deter me.

For all the mess around Rosalind, she spoke easily enough, asking me about my flight down and the hotel where I was staying. When the water had boiled, she looked around for a cup for me, and then walked over to where I was sitting and took one of the dirty ones, put in a tea bag, and poured water in, then brought it back to me. There were toast crumbs floating on the top.

So maybe she was just a very messy person but otherwise OK.

She was talkative too, and I thought I would let her go on to get herself warmed up before we got to the point of my interview. She rambled for quite a while, talking about her career as an actress in movies in the thirties and forties. She mentioned some time with the film director John Ford, who she said had come to her house and taken her out although her mother was not fond of the man.

Was this true? Maybe. I didn't know. I was writing a book about Harrison, not her lover, real or imagined.

"You know, I'm here to find out what I can about your father," I said.

"He left us when I was two."

"Did you ever see him after that?"

"No." She said it as if the conversation was going to end there. I had another moment of unease.

"I think it's time we had something to eat. It's almost lunch." She stood up and walked over to the refrigerator. "This hasn't worked for some time, but I still keep my vegetables in here," she said. The smell of rotted food came out of the fridge when she opened the door. The light was burned out too, so I couldn't see whatever else was in there. I wasn't sure I wanted to. She took out two avocados, very dark. She cut each one in half at the counter, scooped out the pits, and then looked over toward me. She came over and took two dirty saucers, brought them to the counter, and then mashed the avocados with a fork, and brought the plates over.

"Eat," she said.

The avocado was overripe, with many streaks of black mixed in with the dark green. The fork had bumps of old, unwashed food stuck to the tines. I ate, reasoning I couldn't get food poisoning from an avocado, unless there was some ancient bacteria on the saucer below it.

"Tell me about your mother," I said, and she went on at some length about her mother, a saint who had raised her on her own after her father left. They had lived together her mother's whole life.

"And did she talk about your father?" I asked.

"Oh, all the time. While he was still alive, she kept expecting him to come back. I think she hoped for it for decades, right up to the time when we heard he'd died."

"In 1947," I said.

"In 1947. I remember that last letter pretty well, the one that came after we heard he'd died. She said it would be the last one she ever received from him. Then she had to fight to get his death benefit."

A letter. This was a good lead.

By this time we had been talking for quite a while. The side of the house where we sat faced west and the sun was starting to come around, making the air thicker with the smell of old food and ancient dust. Rosalind's speech was getting slower. She sometimes paused between sentences. Maybe she was tired, but I was just starting and I only had a few days to get whatever story I could out of her.

"So your father wrote to your mother?" I asked.

"Oh yes. Regularly."

"For thirty years?"

"Yes. He wrote all the time." She laughed. "Especially when he needed money."

Now I was onto something, but as she said those last words, she blinked a couple of times and then looked at me sharply.

"Who did you say you were again?" she asked.

"I'm a journalist from Toronto."

"And what do you want with me?"

"I'm writing an article about your father."

"So you say. What do you really want?"

I wanted the story. All I ever wanted was the story.

"I have no story. I told you. He left us when I was two years old."

"But maybe there's something in his letters."

"What business do you have asking about his letters? What business do you have being here at all?"

I didn't know quite what to say, and she filled the silence herself.

"Get out of my house."

"Have I said something wrong?"

"I don't need to explain myself to you."

"No, but I hope I haven't offended you."

"Just get out. I showed you the way in. You can find your own way out."

If she looked like a befuddled old lady when I came in, she looked like a dementia patient now. One of her eyelids was drooping but the other eye fixed on me fiercely.

"Can I come back later?"

She didn't answer. I waited a moment to see if she'd had a stroke.

It was blazingly bright outside and I wasn't used to the California heat. If it was this bad in June, what must it be like in July and August? I didn't know what to do. A very old lady had bested me.

I drove around, trying to figure out my next move, or if I even had one. I headed down to the ocean at Newport Beach and walked out on the pier that jutted into the ocean. There were fishermen on the pier and a few surfers off to my right. The view off the end of the pier showed nothing but an expanse of blue all the way to the horizon.

The next morning, I stopped at the supermarket and bought candy and flowers again. Then I had a brilliant idea. I bought a foam cooler and two bags of ice as well as a small carton of ice cream that I nestled inside.

When I knocked on the door, I found her dressed the same way she had been the day before. Her hair was a little matted on one side, so I guessed she had slept in her clothes. But she was smiling at the sight of the flowers. I was getting the picture that she liked gifts.

"What's in the cooler?" she asked.

"Well, you said your fridge was broken, so I bought some ice and ice cream."

Her eyes lit up. "I haven't had ice cream for quite some time. Get in quick. It won't hold up for long."

We returned to the kitchen. My teacup and plate from the day before had not been moved. The remains of the avocado smeared across the bottom of the saucer had turned dark and hard.

She seemed giddy with delight. She opened the cooler once I had put it on the floor and pulled out the carton. She picked two random bowls off the counter and brought the carton over, and we ate the whole thing. When we were done, she put the new flowers in a new vase and opened the box of chocolates and ate two of them.

"You were telling me about some letters from your father yesterday," I said.

"Did you want to see them?"

"Sure."

Sometimes, everything between us was so easy. I felt like she was a mercurial girlfriend and, for the moment, I was getting lucky.

"Come with me."

She led me down the hall. We walked past open doors, one to a bedroom with sheets all piled up on the bed like a nest, another full of newspapers and books, and finally a small study. In the corner of the room was a leather chest, like a smallish pirate's chest. She had me carry the chest back into the room we had been sitting in and we turned our chairs away from the table. I set the chest between us. She opened it up, and I saw it was filled with letters — dozens, maybe even hundreds of them, many written on the onionskin paper that people used to use to save on weight and postage costs.

I looked at the contents, which might be a whole biography in a box, a writer's dream. This was it. I had found my treasure. All I had to do was overcome the dragon that was guarding it. Rosalind reached down and pulled out an envelope that had been sticking up by the edge.

"Look at this," she said. "It's a letter from my mother to my father and it's never been opened. It must have been returned."

She stuck her finger under the corner of the flap and

ripped the letter open. I was feeling protective of the paper already and wished she'd used a knife.

"Oh, my mother's handwriting. It makes me miss her to see it."

"What's the date?" I asked.

"1937."

The letter had been written fifty years earlier and sent to her husband twenty years after he abandoned her. My excitement was rising.

"Can I see it?" I asked.

She didn't pass it over to me. Instead, she began to read, and here are the words as I remember them:

> *Dear Tillson, I dreamt of you again last night. You had finally come back and I was filled with happiness. We held hands and we were walking down the street when you said to me that you needed to go into a store. I waited outside and I watched you through the window, and the shop girl started to chat with you and then she laughed and smiled. It took a long time, and I watched her write something on a piece of paper and hand it over to you and then I realized it was her telephone number. My heart was breaking again, just has it has so many times in the past, and when I awoke, my mood was dour for the whole day. Rosalind asked me what the trouble was after she came in from her picnic with Mr. Ford. Now as to the money, I can't afford to send you any more than fifteen dollars. You can't imagine the pressure we have been under . . .*

The letter went on to talk about financial details. It was fantastic because here I had not only the story of Tillson Lever Harrison, but also the story of the wife whose heart he broke. She was Penelope, steadfast and waiting for her Ulysses twenty years after he left her, and she would be steadfast for another ten years until he died, never having returned after all. And there was also mention of Mr. Ford. Could it really have been John Ford?

Rosalind did not read to the end of the letter. Her voice started to slow. She let her hand drop her side. She seemed a little bored.

"It does make me think of my mother," she said.

"You must have been close."

"We only lived here together for a few years before she died. We lived most of our lives in a house down at Laguna Beach. There used to be a lot of filming down there and I could get to work easily. I haven't seen that house in decades."

I wanted nothing more than to go through the box of letters, but she was speaking so wistfully that I offered to drive her down to Laguna Beach. It was only half an hour away. She agreed. Her directions were very good, but she complained of the bright glare on the road, and I stopped at a gas station to buy her a pair of sunglasses. We drove down a residential street. She had me drive up to a small bungalow, prewar, I guessed, white stucco with slatted glass windows that could be turned up like venetian blinds to let in the breeze. She talked for a bit about her mother giving John Ford hell on the sidewalk outside the house, telling him not to come back while he was still married. Then she had the idea I should take her to a garage where her car was being fixed. The mechanic had advised against it because her Karmann Ghia was so old, but she told him to go ahead. I wondered how an old woman in her condition could drive but this was California, after all. As Joe Gillis said in *Sunset Boulevard*, in a place like this, if you lose your car, it's like having your legs cut off.

By the time I got her home, she was starting to sag. It was midafternoon and I suggested we have tea, but she didn't want any. I tempted her with a couple of chocolates, but they didn't seem to make any difference.

"Do you think I could look at some of the letters?" I asked.

She stared at me for a while.

"Who are you?" she asked. "What are you doing here?"

We went through the same routine as the day before and she threw me out.

I was disappointed, but not as much as I had been the day before. Now I knew she was crazy, but only in the afternoon. If I could get her in the morning, I would be fine. And I also knew everything I needed was in a chest on the floor of her house. I would be back for it again the next day.

The next morning I came with flowers, chocolates, ice, ice cream, fudge, cheese and crackers as well as a couple of bottles of Coca-Cola. I needed her to be filled with sugar and caffeine and I needed to act fast.

Thankfully, she had changed her shirt, but nothing else in house was different. The chest of letters was where she had left it, with the lid open. My salvation was in there and I needed to get it.

At first, she wanted to go through the letters with me but all the treats I'd brought distracted her, and I began to pick letters at random, looking for the oldest one first. I picked up a single sheet written in black ink that had turned brown with time. Harrison was writing from Mexico in an undated letter that must have arrived around 1914. I would need to find the envelope if it was still in the chest. He talked of being the chief medical officer to Pancho Villa, the Mexican revolutionary. The letter was a mixture of the banal and the dramatic, of his temporary imprisonment when Villa suspected him of being a spy. This one letter alone was filled with tantalizing information, but I knew there was more. In another letter I found mention of Dr. Sun Yat-sen, the Chinese father of revolution, and then in yet another the story of an escape from a British ship taking him from Turkey back to the U.K. He jumped ship in Morocco, literally, and swam half a mile to shore, where he climbed out of the water with nothing but his wet clothes and his wits to find a way to his next adventure.

Harrison's story had been so full of rumours of these events that I'd expected the truth would diminish them. But the opposite was happening. I had before me the traces of an adventurer who seemed to have a knack for picking all the hot spots of the first half of the twentieth century and inserting himself into them. I took a few notes but I'd only gone through four or five letters when I realized it would be impossible to note everything inside the chest. I needed to make copies in order to study the material over time.

I looked up to Rosalind. She had sat down at the glass-topped table, eaten ice cream and chocolates and now she had cut through the plastic package of cheese and was breaking off bits of it with her hands and putting the bits on crackers. If she kept eating the way she was going, she was going to end up with a bad stomach ache.

"These letters are really something," I said. I had been crouched over the box and now I sat upright in my chair across from the glass-topped table.

"Uh huh."

"I wonder if I could make copies of them?"

"Go ahead. Make all the notes you want."

"There's too much here, though. I'd like to make some photocopies."

She paused in the middle of delivering another cheese-topped cracker to her mouth.

"Those letters don't leave this house," she said, and delivered the next bite. The sound of the cracker crunching in her mouth was intolerable.

I was flying out the next night so I didn't have much time. "We could go together," I said.

"It's too bright outside."

I didn't know what to do, so I picked out a letter at random and began to read it. Harrison was ship's doctor on an American cruiser during World War II. This was not exactly scintillating in itself but it was a discovery that added another piece to the mosaic of his life. I copied the name of the ship, both excited at the information but practically ready to explode with rage at the closeness of the material I could not copy.

"Did I ever tell you about my political convictions?" Rosalind had stopped eating for the moment. There were crumbs on her chin. Part of me wanted to tell her or to wipe them away myself and part of me wanted to say nothing and leave them there. I said nothing. She said she was a staunch Republican.

"Oh?"

I wondered why she had chosen to say this to me at that

moment. The sun was coming around to our side of the house again. She had left the new cooler lid open and I could hear the last chunk of ice settle. There was no use trying to feed her anything else. She had been eating nonstop.

She would turn on me soon. I knew it was coming. Then I would have to leave the place and start the whole routine again the next morning. Would it really be so bad just to pick up the box and walk out with it? She would certainly try to stop me but what could a frail old lady do? I didn't think she was capable of calling the police and the neighbours must know she was crazy.

Time was running out.

I wondered again why she had told me about being a Republican. Republicans tended to be in favour of the NRA and the right to bear arms. She might have been old, but if she was a Republican, she might also have a pistol tucked away somewhere.

Of course, if I knocked down her chair, she would struggle to get up from the floor. I could close the lid of the chest and be out of there before she gathered herself up.

So this was how people found themselves doing things they would not ordinarily do. All it took was to have something you really wanted and an impediment that could be overcome at a price.

I thought my dark thoughts.

For some reason, the Beatles song jumped into my head, something about Mother Superior jumping the gun. I wasn't thinking much about the gun, really. I was thinking about Mother Superior, who was transformed into Mother Leone, my elementary school teacher.

I was raised by nuns in my Catholic school, and unlike some who had been hurt by their Catholic education, or who hated the memory of it, I remembered it fondly, if ironically. All those processions around the school hallways with plaster saints, all the adoration of the host in the days before Easter, the peculiar smell of incense and trying to catch drops when the priest walked around the church flinging holy water onto the congregation.

Now Mother Leone stood prominent in my mind as Rosalind wet her fingertip and picked up cracker crumbs off the glass tabletop. Mother Leone had been all sweetness and understanding, in her gold-rimmed glasses and face framed by the white and black cowl. Sweet, yes, but fierce too. And Mother Leone was a lion for justice.

The ghost of Mother Leone roared in my mind. Maybe it was the gold-rimmed glasses. Rosalind Paquette wore them too, and she was some version of the fierce nun now down on her luck.

I sighed. If I couldn't kill Rosalind, what else could I do?

"Who are you again?" Rosalind asked.

※

I was beaten, but not defeated.

It was 1988. There were no portable photocopiers at the time. In the hours that remained in the afternoon, I thumbed through the telephone directory and called around. Nobody rented copiers but a salesman at a store would let me have a smallish one for twenty-four hours if I put down a deposit of a thousand dollars in cash. I called Snaige in Toronto, and she wired me the cash that I picked up at a Western Union office. Then I met the salesman at the back of his warehouse, where I gave him the thousand on the loading dock, wondering if I wouldn't be stuck with a photocopier that I couldn't bring back to Toronto the next day.

By six o'clock I was set, but at eight o'clock I had a sudden insight and found a hardware store where I bought a piece of equipment, just in case.

I showed up early the next morning with my third cooler and bags of M&Ms, potato chips, cheese, crackers, dried fruit, and beef jerky. Rosalind didn't seem surprised at all to see me. She let me in and I made a few trips back to the car, finally walking in with the heavy photocopier that forced me to use all my strength to keep from dropping it.

"What's that?" she asked.

"A copier. You said I could bring one."

"I did?"

"Would you like some potato chips?"

I knelt on the floor and set myself up and, sure enough, the photocopier cord had three prongs but the wall plugs had only two holes. I had anticipated the problem and bought an adapter at the hardware store the night before.

Not only had I been a Catholic boy, I'd also been a Boy Scout. I was prepared.

It would still be tight. I had hundreds of pages to copy along with the envelopes, and the machine moved with agonizing slowness. But I had brought such a variety of treats that the consumption of them would permit me to finish the job.

Even so, it was a stretch. As I was coming to the end of my job, I looked up at Rosalind. The bag of beef jerky had defeated her. She chewed for a while, but didn't have the teeth to gnaw past one piece. The M&Ms were gone, though.

And then she gave me that look. It didn't matter. I had all I needed.

※

In the end, it was not a biography but a five-part CBC radio play I wrote on the life of Dr. Tillson Lever Harrison. Every couple of years, though, I'd get a call from some writer eager to do his full biography. To each of aspiring biographers I'd say what Ted Allan said to me, "Find another subject. Tillson Lever Harrison's story has broken the heart of more than one writer."

As for Rosalind Paquette, whenever I found myself in California, I'd phone her and she was cordial, as if she remembered me. But I had no reason to go over there. She lived for another eighteen years, dying at age ninety-eight. The papers and dirty dishes must have accumulated over all that time, and I sometimes wonder if anyone looked into the chest of letters and dreamed of writing the biography of the elusive Dr. Tillson Lever Harrison.

1988
I FEEL *the* EARTH MOVE
under MY FEET

I was standing in front of my first-year journalism students, reading aloud the rules of engagement in my English class, when a tiny coloured arc flew by on the periphery of my vision. I stopped to look down and saw that a young woman at the front of the class was clipping her painted toenails. I watched, fascinated, as she unselfconsciously worked her way across one foot and moved on to the next. No one else in the class remarked upon this, so I made a note to add "clipping toenails" onto the list of prohibited activities in my class.

The rules of behaviour were in flux. Necklines dropped, so I looked into the middle distance whenever a seated female asked me a question about her work on the page. The college now permitted students to eat in classes; however, after noisy cellophane-covered salads appeared, along with salad dressing squirted across neighbouring desks, I unilaterally forbade eating meals in my room. Texting didn't exist yet. Candies were OK except for lollipops because the sight of a stick wobbling up and down in a student's mouth was distracting to me. Without a doctor's note, anyone who missed a test got zero.

I didn't want to be a tyrant, but I could take nothing for granted. Students believed anything not expressly forbidden must be acceptable, which was why I published a list of pro-hibited activities and added to them whenever something new happened. Such as clipping toenails in class.

I was trying to be Mr. Chips, firm but as entertaining and understanding as possible in a class where I taught grammar as well as creative writing. Students had the right to call for a time out occasionally. Whenever it looked like the difference between a noun clause and an adverb phrase was killing them, they could ask me for a story, and I'd break for five minutes to tell the tale of the haunted house or the mouse in the rocket or my near failure with Rosalind Paquette.

Full-time teaching as well as magazine and radio freelanc-ing and a young family with two boys were all eating into my writing time, but much to my surprise, I found I liked teaching.

Why should anything change?

Snaige and I had rediscovered Wasaga Beach, the place we ethnic kids had fled until we had children of our own in the mid-eighties. The shallow lake was appealing, and our parents gave us free lodging and helped take care of the children. It was not exactly the heroic life I'd imagined for myself when I was young, but it was a good life and I knew we were lucky to have it.

Big Al had a cottage two doors over. I'd known him in uni-versity when we played a lot of poker. He was a political junkie and a PR specialist and could be counted on to say something provocative or insightful while offering ice-cold vodka shots. He threw gigantic parties that spilled out onto the cottage streets and sometimes ended up with police cruisers arriving to keep the peace. And like a lot of neighbours in this ethnic ghetto of a beach town, he was Lithuanian.

Big Al asked me to come over one day when my son was taking his afternoon nap and Snaige was breastfeeding his younger brother. Al wanted me to look at something. He flipped a tape into his VCR.

I knew the place he showed, in Vilnius, because I'd been there a couple of times as a tourist to visit relatives separated by the war. To get there I'd taken a train from West Berlin and watched the search dogs crawl under the cars and the armed guard walk over the top as we rolled into East Berlin and then even deeper into Cold War lands. Warsaw was a grey town, and things got greyer as I travelled further east into my family's part of the Soviet Union. Restrictions were legion, visits outside the capital forbidden, and even long-lost relatives spoke with great circumspection.

In the video Big Al showed me, I saw several hundred people demonstrating on the seventieth anniversary of the declaration of Lithuanian independence. I could not believe they had gotten away with it. The Soviet Union occupied Lithuania during the war, killed some and deported tens of thousands of others before transforming the place into a sullen police state. Demonstrations were not supposed to happen, and if they did arrests followed.

News moved more slowly then, and not much of this had been reported in the American or Canadian press. The world I inhabited had not changed in my entire life. It had never occurred to me that it ever would. The Cold War would go on forever, even if it had become a little boring over the last decade, the concern of high-level politicians and Eastern Europeans and no one else. The causes of my generation were South Africa, California grape pickers, and eventually

Nicaragua. The Soviet Union was something like North Korea today, but considerably less grotesque because Mikhail Gorbachev was talking reform, and with his fedora and rain-coat, he was coming across like a Russian Frank Sinatra. He was doing communism his way. Regrets, he'd have a few.

When I stepped out of Big Al's cottage, I looked about me on the street. The shady and pleasant resort town remained unchanged. Soon my sons would awake from their afternoon nap, and they and my wife and I would make our way down to Georgian Bay for a swim while one of us cradled the baby. Everything seemed the same, but nothing was the same.

I wrote a short letter to Anne Collins, then the editor at *Saturday Night* magazine. The magazine couldn't cover foreign expenses, but she would pay for a political piece and George Galt would let me write a travel piece to help cover my costs.

Back at Humber College, in the middle of the semester, my dean was not thrilled to see me take off, but I found a supply teacher to replace me and wrote off a couple of weeks of lost income.

※

I approached Moscow's Sheremetyevo Airport under late October skies. Vast patches of birches interspersed with lakes looked like something out of a black and white movie. A man in a peaked military cap studied my currency declaration, visa, passport, and tickets carefully. He asked me to take off my glasses as he studied my face, even though I had glasses on in the passport photo. There wasn't much reform going on in this place.

Then it was out into the great hall, a vast hangar-like room filled with an assortment of babushkas, men in uniform, and dodgy characters in leather jackets. One of them came up to me and told me he was my driver. I wasn't sure how he knew, but I took his word for it and got into his rattling car to bounce through the potholes on the way to the domestic airport, where he dropped me off.

If the international airport was a hangar, this airport was like a train station out of *Doctor Zhivago*. Whole gypsy-looking families were asleep among bundles on the floor and masses of people stood at ticket windows where passengers bent low to shout at stone-faced ticket sellers. A long line stood at the cafeteria to buy glasses of thick cream, twin slices of black bread curling as they dried on saucers, and eternal dishes of herring and onions that Khrushchev probably passed by on the last time he was through.

I was disoriented and lost. I wandered the crowded room looking at various signs whose Russian I could not decipher. Then I came upon a blond wooden door with the words *Intourist* crudely stencilled on it. All foreign visitors flew Intourist. I opened the door to a compact waiting room like a fifties hotel lobby, with couches and a couple of palm trees and a receptionist who spoke English. I could drink champagne and eat caviar while I waited.

But the first-class treatment ended when it came time to board the plane. A bus took us out to the dark runway, and we waited there interminably until the door on the rear end of a plane dropped down and we were invited to get on. Tickets had been issued randomly, so couples and friends immediately sat together despite seat numbers. Arguments followed until a stewardess, like some prison guard out of the women's gulag, yelled at everyone, and the passengers meekly dropped into seats like disorderly convicts beaten into good behaviour. The pilot boarded last, pulled the door shut behind him, and then walked to the front of the plane. He pushed aside a curtain and seemed to place a key in the ignition. We flew off as if we were in a car just pulling away from the curb. Aeroflot flights tended to be bumpy and alarming, and this was especially true when we landed in Vilnius and taxied past old planes, some burnt out, as if passing through an aviation junkyard.

The chimneys of the baroque city of Vilnius were feeding streams of smoke into low-lying mist. The city was transforming itself, both physically and politically. When I had first visited in 1975, the seventeenth-century houses were in various states of decay and elaborate nineteenth-century mansions seemed sooty and grim. Now the city was being excavated, renovated, and restored while historians were beginning to rummage through archives and interview former deportees who had been silent for thirty years.

And the streets were full of activity.

※

Vytautas Bogušis was barely thirty but cut from an old-school dissident model. He'd been fighting the regime since before the Gorbachev thaw. He was lean and hollow-cheeked and lived in a ground floor flat in a courtyard in the old part of town. He told me the rest of the apartments in the complex were empty, except for a couple where the KGB listeners kept track of everything he said. I closed my mouth abruptly and he laughed and said it was OK. This chain-smoker with ulcers was used to being harassed. His wife was endlessly warned at work to divorce him and his young daughter was made to stand and take abuse from the teacher in school, all because of what her father did. And what he did, among other things, was help organize that first demonstration I had seen back at Big Al's cottage.

What struck me most about him was his uncompromising refusal to back down. Lithuania was occupied. The occupiers had no right in law to run their regime. His wife and daughter's sufferings were collateral damage that could not be avoided in the service of truth.

He worked as a theatre hand but his real work was shaming the regime, Gorbachev's fashionable reputation be damned. I watched him lighting up yet another smoke and admired his resolution, and then I looked to his wife and daughter, who seemed harried and resigned.

Lithuania was in turmoil and transition, but in 1988 it was far from free yet. It was still illegal for a foreigner to leave the capital without express permission, but I had a local driver take me a few hours up to Šiauliai, a provincial capital, to meet with a group of priests who were pushing for reform. On the way back along the highway, otherwise empty that night, a car pulled up behind us and tailed us with high beams on. It pulled up beside us and the driver looked over at us and waved and smiled. Then it pulled ahead of us and slowed dramatically.

"The KGB is sending us a message," my driver said.

Once it was clear the message was delivered, the car sped away.

As in Poland, the Catholic Church was a locus of resistance. I drove out to the town of Merkinė, where one priest told the story of how he had been recruited by the KGB to spy upon the students in the local seminary. In that very seminary, I met Father Sigitas Tamkevičius, who had run a samizdat church chronicle of human rights abuses.

The country was roiling and the unsteady communist government was beginning to give up its game of whack-a-mole.

My in-country guides and friends were a pair of artists, Mindaugas and Saulė, and in this small country with very few degrees of separation, they had gone to school with the daughter of Vytautas Brazauskas, the new chair of the Central Committee of the Lithuanian Communist Party. A couple of calls and the next day I was walking down the dimly lit halls of the Central Committee headquarters, where occasional pairs of officials lingered in doorways to measure me as I made my way into the chairman's office.

I was the first Western reporter to get access, and I was being allowed to ask questions of the bluff and beefy charmer, a man who looked as if he had just stepped down from a tractor in a Soviet-realist film. Unlike old-time officials, he seemed reasonable and open and answered expertly, siding with Gorbachev, promoting reform, urging caution and respect for the Soviet constitution. Of course, he had been part of the Central Committee that helped harass dissidents like Vytautas Bogušis, but now he was a new man, a modern politician.

I don't know what I would have done without Mindaugas, who kept helping me out. I was a lousy photographer and compensated by taking hundreds of shots for *Saturday Night*, hoping that a few would be publishable. When my camera lens froze in the premature cold, he taught me to keep the thing under my coat and against my body until I needed to pull it out.

I was curious to see how much I could get away with in an effort to measure the loosening of the regime, so I had Mindaugas take me to a chilly outdoor marketplace. We walked around the food stalls until we came to a place where a Georgian orange merchant also had a bottle of Armenian cognac set on the table beside him, offered for sale at six rubles. With Mindaugas as a translator into Russian, I asked him if he would accept American dollars and, if so, how many for the bottle.

He said two dollars, which was the right black market rate at the time, more than three times better than the official exchange rate foreigners were supposed to adhere to. I handed over two bills, and the Georgian suddenly lifted his arm and waved over a man in a uniform. This caught the attention of the crowd, and others began to drift over. I thought things were going to turn out badly. Maybe I had stepped beyond the bounds of evolving reform by making this public black market deal.

The uniformed man walked over, all brass buttons and a peaked cap, and he spoke with the Georgian. The crowd around us grew.

"What's going on?" I asked Mindaugas.

"He wants to check if the bills are real."

The uniformed man rubbed one and held it up to the light. We were practically in a theatre at this point, with dozens of people milling around the spectacle. Then he did the same with the second one and said the something to the Georgian.

"He says the second bill is counterfeit."

The mob in the marketplace jeered as if a thief had been found.

I wanted to get out of there as fast as I could. I asked for the dollars back, but the Georgian just wanted me to try another bill, and this second bill passed muster. The Georgian handed me the bottle of cognac and we pushed our way through the crowd.

Relieved, back in Mindaugas's apartment, we opened the bottle to celebrate having gotten away with it.

"What kind of policeman was the man in the uniform?" I asked.

"He was no policeman. He was a train conductor. The Georgian considered him a man of experience, someone who'd seen the world, so he wanted advice."

"Why was that?"

"He thought you might be trying to cheat him."

The sums seemed laughably small to me. Why would I bother to cheat someone for so little money?

We sipped at the cognac, and Mindaugas's grimace reflected my own shock. It wasn't brandy. It was some kind of unidentified spirit coloured with tea. It turned out the Georgian didn't want us to cheat him before he could cheat us with his counterfeit liquor.

❈

When I got back to Toronto, I wrote my pieces for the magazine and I travelled to Lithuania again for CBC Radio and for *Reader's Digest*, a magazine I hadn't really taken seriously until it took me seriously. I kept a passport with me at all times in case I needed to go suddenly and became a kind of intermediary for Daniel Schwartz and Linden MacIntyre at CBC-TV's

The Journal, where I provided background information or contacts or phoned through on the unreliable phone lines to Lithuania.

The youth who had tried to escape the beer barrel polka of his ethnic parents became Mr. Lithuania in Canada, a pundit on radio and TV, a sort of expert about a place no one had paid any attention to for over forty years.

✖

While the Soviet Union roiled, my English classes at Humber College rolled on as smoothly as Old Man River, with just an occasional splash.

One late winter afternoon, when the day classes had pretty much ended and the halls were empty before night classes began, one of my students asked to stay behind after the others had left. He wanted me to know, he said, that if he ever scored a low grade in a class, he went crazy. I walked over to look at my grade book. I told him he'd missed a test, and thus scored zero on it.

He told me he had a good excuse.

"Try me," I said, sure I had heard it all.

He handed me a sheet of paper, a police form. He'd missed my test because he'd been busy being charged with attempted murder at the time.

It was the best excuse I'd ever heard. I let him do a make-up test. Subsequently, his lawyer was very good about calling to get homework for classes he missed while in court.

1989-1991

THE CHURCH BASEMENT
versus the KREMLIN

My job in the operation was to sniff the vice-president when he arrived. I was to assess the acceptability of his clothes when he landed at the airport in Toronto and then brief him about the Ottawa meeting with the Canadian government. Joana was waiting in Ottawa, all set to buy a new shirt if his was frayed, and the two Als — Big Al and Tall Al — and Tom were dealing with the media. There was no lack of media. All the Canadian newspapers and networks wanted information, and the *New York Times* led the American pack.

It was January 1989 and Lithuania was trying to break away from the Soviet Union. Canada and America didn't like it because the separatists were going to undermine Gorbachev. Five church basement ethnics from Toronto were going to do our best to bring the Canadian government along. Hundreds more were doing their bit across North America.

We five had been kids together in Lithuanian Saturday school (much reviled because it deprived us of morning cartoons); Lithuanian Boy Scouts (and my sub-specialty, the Lithuanian Sea Scouts); Lithuanian folk dance ensembles; or church basement basketball leagues (playing Ukrainians, Latvians, and Estonians — in effect, the Vanished Nations League).

186

We grew up and moved on. Joana and Tall Al were lawyers, Big Al a PR specialist, Tom a provincial government mandarin, and me — a college English teacher and scribbler. Our church basement childhoods were a rich source of amusement in our adult lives, a kind of ethnic joke to all of us whenever we met at weddings or funerals.

Then the Soviet Union started to crumble, and the church basement ethnics rose up. We were to help Estonia, Latvia, and Lithuania tear themselves away from the Soviet Union that had swallowed them in 1939.

The scraps of information we'd retained from our Saturday school days and our subsequent contact with Lithuanian political activists made us experts sought out by the CBC and the *Globe and Mail* for our knowledge of the mice that roared so loudly the world order was now at risk. The politicians in Ottawa liked their ethnics to do funny dances and cook exotic foods but not upset international relations.

We five and the rest did indeed want to upset international relations.

We'd asked the unrecognized Lithuanian government to send a representative to help us pressure the politicians, and their envoy was Bronius Kuzmickas, a professor of the history of philosophy who'd just been appointed vice-president. We were his handlers, making sure he did not make the wrong impression. Those who came from the Soviet Union, we knew, did not always make the right impression. It was important that he smell good, look good, and sound good for the Ottawa press. We were a combination beauty salon and charm school.

Canada did not yet recognize his vice-presidency, so we could not get VIP treatment for him at the airport, but I was allowed to go into the baggage carousel room when the plane landed, and there I saw a tired man who had travelled from Vilnius to Moscow and then to Toronto over the last thirty-six hours. He looked like an absent-minded professor, with large eyeglasses and slightly long, curly grey hair. He was standing by the carousel in a dirty white trench coat, waiting for his bag. I went up and introduced myself and he shook my hand.

I leaned in close and sniffed. There was no deodorant, it seemed, in the Soviet Union, and some of the visitors we had had in the past had worn the same sweaty shirt for thirty-six hours. But the vice-president passed the nose test. As for looks, his shirt and suit looked fine, if a little dowdy in the Soviet mode, but the trench coat looked bad and the bags under his eyes showed how tired he was.

He was cordial and professorial but he was going to have to make a big impression in Ottawa. We had a couple of hours to kill until his next flight, so I took him to the lounge and ran through a list of thirty questions the media might ask him.

In the lounge, he wanted to order a beer but I forbade it. I reasoned he had been travelling and would be tired and a beer would relax him too much. I didn't want him relaxed. I wanted him sharp. I ordered a coffee for him and, much to my surprise, he took my advice. Then I took out my questions.

"What will you say," I said, "when they ask you why Lithuania wants to declare independence from the Soviet Union?"

He thought about the question for an agonizing four or five seconds and then started a history lesson that began in the fifteenth century and sounded like it would be delivered in real time.

I had a vision of TV cameras turning off, of politicians turning away, of the Soviet Union hanging strong for another century.

I stopped him and told him he would need to have a sound bite that ran no longer than twenty seconds. He protested that twenty seconds to explain the aspirations of millions of people were not enough.

It was moronic to expect such brevity, he said. I welcomed him to the continent of morons. I told him that twenty seconds were all he had.

I am not sure which one of us was more unlikely in our role. I was an aspiring novelist and a college English teacher giving lessons in public relations, and he was a philosophy professor who would have to sway the media in order to sway the people of Canada in order to sway the politicians.

We were out of our depth, but we improvised.

When it came time to leave the lounge and get on the plane to Ottawa, Mr. Vice-President stood, lifted his briefcase, and put his coat on his arm.

"You can leave the coat here," I said.

"I don't understand."

"The coat is too thin for Ottawa. It will be freezing up there. We'll get you a new coat."

His coat looked pathetic. Wrong image. He left the trench coat behind.

Joana met us in a limousine in Ottawa. "We need to get him a coat," I said.

"There's no time. We have to head directly to the West Block. The dinner has begun and the two Als and Tom have arranged media."

It was frigid in Ottawa, a good minus ten with wind. If the vice-president wasn't going to be wearing a coat, neither was I. Let the Canadian media think that Lithuanians didn't put on coats until it hit minus fifteen. We strode out from the car, where a furious wind whipped my hair and his, and the three of us walked down the long corridor to the hall where the ministers of justice and finance were guests among the hundreds of Canadians of Estonian, Latvian, and Lithuanian background. I'd had three hours with my student and now I would see how well he'd perform.

As we walked along, down at the far end of the grand corridor, I saw five, six, seven camera lights pop on and a bevy of journalists thrust their microphones out.

Bronius Kuzmickas, the history of philosophy prof, straightened his back, adapted his stride to seem determined, and walked into the half circle.

"Why do your people want to upset the most liberal leader that Moscow has ever seen in order to seek independence?" the CBC asked.

"We want freedom. We lost it once, and we mean to get it back now. Everyone wants freedom, don't you think?"

I marvelled at him. He took half a dozen questions, answering each one firmly and briefly, and then we said we needed to go into the hall.

There, the crowd rose in standing ovation as he walked in. The MC ceded the microphone to him as Bronius Kuzmickas stepped onto the podium.

"I have come from a long way," he said, "to seek your help. The people of our nations have been imprisoned for too long."

I was translating for him, and the speech he gave lasted

fifteen minutes and was worthy of the liberation rhetoric of Martin Luther King. When it was over, various Important People wanted to speak to him and he had enough English to handle private conversation, so I sat down at a banquet table to eat something. I didn't recognize the woman sitting across the table from me.

"Quite the speech," she said.

"Think so?" I was tired now that my job was more or less over and I wasn't paying close attention but I listened to her talk for a while. Later I learned it was Kim Campbell, who would go on to be prime minister for a brief period, but back then I could barely tell one politician from another.

The stores were closed by the time the dinner was over, so we went straight to the hotel in an entourage of half a dozen people. None of us wore coats. The next day, there was an early press conference at the media centre across from the parliament buildings. It was still very cold, possibly worse than the day before, but when we stepped out, none of us was wearing a coat.

The five of us who accompanied him looked like something out of a heist movie. We strode bare-headed, bare-handed, and shivering into the media centre, where Bronius Kuzmickas worked his magic again.

When we finally had enough time, he and I walked into The Bay to buy him a coat. I showed him sober wool coats and demure cashmere, but he leaned toward a kind of shiny padded material that made him look like a walking quilt.

"Don't buy that one," I said.

"I want something modern."

He put his foot down. He had outgrown me. The vice-president of Lithuania would choose his own damned coat. He looked like the Michelin Man on a diet, but he carried it off well.

※

When President Vytautas Landsbergis showed up some months later, Lithuania had declared its independence, but the Soviet Union was having none of it. He was coming to meet the prime minister of Canada and I was again assigned to be the Lithuanian's handler.

By this time, the press was in a slump on the subject of the Soviet Union, so it was hard to get any media attention. Canadian media were like high school cool kids — their attention slipped easily. President Vytautas Landsbergis was, if anything, more professorial that his vice-president, more deliberate in his speech, and with an unfortunate little tic — a laugh that sounded like something from the mouth of an evil cartoon character. He also had relatively good English, so he wanted to carry on without an interpreter, but we had convinced him that interpretation was a ploy. He would have more time to think about his answers if he understood them in English and could then wait for the Lithuanian translation to finish.

He flew into Montreal to do a church basement appearance among the Lithuanian Canadians. There was hardly any media there at all and not much interest that I could scare up. I had convinced the reluctant CBC Radio show *As It Happens* to do at least a pre-interview with him in order to see if he was acceptable to them. In those days before ubiquitous cell phones, I had to take the president up a back staircase from the Montreal church basement to talk to a CBC Radio producer who was not all that interested in what he had to say. She declined a subsequent interview.

People were now bored by the story. Morons have short attention spans.

This was not turning out as brilliantly as my last assignment with the vice-president. But by now, the Canadian government was beginning to be at least lukewarm in its relations with Lithuania, which was better than the freezing receptions of months earlier. The government specified that the RCMP was to drive President Landsbergis to Ottawa from Montreal. My job was to sit with him in the back seat and train him the way I had trained Bronius Kuzmickas.

We started off late and I had to ride in a separate car at first because the president was taking a briefing from someone else. But the entourage of six cars stopped at a windy, dark crossroads, and I joined the president in the back seat and we continued on to Ottawa. He knew me slightly from my earlier journalistic assignment with *Saturday Night* magazine, so I felt we had some kind of minimal rapport.

The two Mounties in the front seat played their roles perfectly by looking bulky and driving without making conversation. I took out my clipboard and a small flashlight and explained what I was going to do. But then I made a fatal mistake. I mentioned that for all I knew, the car was bugged, but there was no need to worry about it because nothing I was going to say was secret in any way.

I had miscalculated. I had forgotten that a man who came from a totalitarian state did not take lightly to being bugged.

"If they ask you why you are seeking independence, what will you say?" I asked.

President Landsbergis looked at me through his gold-rimmed glasses and above his neat goatee and said nothing. He eyes betrayed nothing either.

I repeated the question.

Still nothing.

"OK, then," I said. "Let's try the next questions."

And so it went, though all thirty questions. Not only did he say nothing to the questions but having been forewarned about a bugged car, he said nothing more all the way to the Château Laurier in Ottawa.

I was a PR hack wannabe failure.

The big event that next day was a meeting with Prime Minister Mulroney and Joe Clark, who was minister of Foreign Affairs. Our entourage kept on being beset by minor problems. Tall Al lost a button on his double-breasted jacket and since I was the only one with a needle and thread repair kit, I sewed it back on for him but managed to sew his wallet shut in his breast pocket. None of us had had much sleep, and when we walked into the prime minister's anteroom, the primitive cell phone in Tom's briefcase went off. None of us was used to cell phones yet and the phone continued to ring off and on as we wondered what kind of security apparatus was malfunctioning somewhere.

I was the only Canadian of the entourage to enter the meeting because I had been asked by the prime minister's office to act as his official translator. It was a job beyond my capabilities because my Lithuanian language skills were reasonable, but not great. Encouraged by my friends and family, I took the assignment and spent the most fretful hour of my life in that office. Unlike most translators, whose memory seemed to be very good, I could not listen to a minute or two's worth of speech and then remember enough of it to repeat it in translation. I had to speak just a few seconds behind the prime minister, listening for what he was saying and simultaneously translating what he had said a moment before.

The Lithuanian president sought Canadian support, some of it very dramatic, and the two ministers were supportive in spirit but declined to make the bold gestures Landsbergis wanted. I was unaccustomed to being in seats of power and had never been a very big fan of either of the Canadian politicians, but I was filled with admiration for their ability to stickhandle a delicate situation. In my heart, I was pushing for Lithuanian independence and Canada's support, but I was the prime minister's man in this case, a temporary servant of Canada, and that was where my allegiance lay. I was astonished to be in the role at all when I would ordinarily have been in a classroom at that hour, standing before students and teaching the importance of punctuation.

It was nerve-wracking, but it was also bliss then to be alive.

History is full of tragedies; it is also full of comedies.

As the meeting was breaking up and everyone was standing around, Prime Minister Mulroney tried to make a small joke. He explained in a roundabout way that President Vytautas Landsbergis was on the news a lot, and his face was becoming as well known as that of Geraldo Rivera.

I knew a direct translation would be incomprehensible, so I broke my oath to translate without improvisation and said the following:

"The Canadian prime minister has a made an untranslatable

joke about Geraldo Rivera and he will be disappointed if you do not laugh."

President Landsbergis chuckled appreciatively.

⚒

My work on the Lithuanian independence file was hectic, but spotty. Sometimes the events were funny, and then they were not.

One January evening in 1991 I came home from tobogganing with my two boys to find my phone ringing off the hook and three different news services were asking me to comment on the tanks that had crushed or shot dead fourteen civilian volunteers and wounded seven hundred others defending the television tower in Vilnius. A flight of Soviet commandos had landed at the airport and a pro-communist group named itself the ruling committee of Lithuania with the intention of bringing it back into the Soviet Union.

I did radio shows and I helped out at CBC Television, where I managed to get a line into the besieged parliament buildings where the defenders of independence had built barricades and volunteers had made Molotov cocktails in the expectation of imminent attack. Those professorial types I had so brazenly advised about sound bites in Ottawa were refusing to give up their dreams of independence. The president's aide, who I managed to reach by phone, said he expected to die defending the parliament building that night. Luckily, Tom was in an apartment across the street and I phoned him regularly for updates.

The Soviet Union was sinking and we weren't sure what it

might take down with it. As all this was going on, I was teaching English classes at Humber College and taking calls at all hours. I'm not sure what my colleagues must have thought. The three I shared an office with all heard me talking to the one person I knew in Paris with uncertain ties to arms dealers about getting weapons into Lithuania if necessary. Someone had managed to buy a ship-to-shore radio that worked by satellite in case the lights went out in Lithuania and a last message needed to be sent out to the free world.

At dinner parties in Toronto, my friends tut-tutted over what might happen to world stability if separatists like the Lithuanians had their way. Others claimed we should let the Soviets have their sphere of influence, notwithstanding the attempt of those under the sphere to escape from it. In the literary world, where I played a minor role, a new generation of hipsters couldn't have cared less.

And then it was the summer of 1991. I was up at a remote off-the-grid cabin with my wife and children, scraping the peeling paint off the windows. Keith walked over from the neighbouring cottage to say he'd heard on the radio that there had been a putsch in Moscow. I motored out of the place and drove to Bala to pump the pay phone full of coins and find out what was going on. By then, there was not much for me to do. I waited and watched with everyone else.

Nobody was laughing now.

In September of 1991, the Soviet Union ceased to exist. In that same month, Canada officially recognized Lithuania's independence and I received a call from Ottawa, inviting me to travel with finance minister Michael Wilson to establish diplomatic relations with Lithuania.

It was to be my last hurrah, but the plan was squelched. I asked my dean if I could get away for a week, but she said I'd been away from Humber College too much and forbade it. The ministry of external affairs was willing to up the ante by going over my dean's head to the president of the college, but I declined because I knew I would have to work under my dean for years to come.

Besides, the moment had passed. I went back to writing novels. The first couple of years were hard. Nobody called from media or the government any longer. It was actually quite dull. But Doris Lessing once said in a TV interview that a writer needs to be a little bored in order to write stories. And that was what I was ever after. A little bored.

As to Big Al and Tall Al, Joana and Tom, we have drifted apart into our own lives. I run across them from time to time in the church basement when there's a funeral or a wedding. But otherwise, we don't see each other any longer. There is no need.

2009–2013
DINNER *with* DEMENTIA

As we began to lose my mother-in-law to dementia, dinner at her kitchen table became one of the casualties of her decline.

That kitchen had once been her entire realm and her chair at the table a kind of throne — from there she could see down the hall and right out onto the street as she talked on the phone to her friends and relatives. That door was thrown open by her husband and children, her brothers and their families, neighbours and friends, and eventually her son and daughter-in-law and grandchildren, all charging down the hall to eat.

She fed us all, but she was never a good cook. Conversation mattered more to her than food. She was fascinated by every-day life in her small neighbourhood universe: the children she saw on the street on her way to No Frills, the dogs and cats, the birds at the feeder, and above all the parade of family and friends at that kitchen table, that miraculous kitchen table that could shrink to hold two or four or expand for eight or twelve, depending on who walked in through the door.

That kitchen was a point of gravity, with family members stopping by before moving on to evening activities; it was a daycare where the grandchildren stayed for days at a time; it was a crisis centre for disasters big and small, from tanks moving during the collapse of the Soviet Union to the crushing of our dog under the wheels of a car on the street outside; and eventually it was a sick room for a son who lived nearby and came for solace as he declined, and then for a husband who began to fail and needed to be shepherded out of this world.

As the grandchildren grew older and the friends began to die, the door opened less and less often. Some days when I walked past her house on my way from the subway, I could see her sitting alone by her table through the perpetually open screen door, maybe peeling an apple or drinking tea — pleased to talk if I came through the door, but equally willing to wave happily, knowing I didn't have time for her now.

None of us had much time.

As the months passed, she became a little confused, not recognizing one or another of the grandchildren, or getting dressed at night to wait at the door for military transport to go to Afghanistan to help her grandson who really was fighting there with the Canadian armed forces. We had someone move in with her to help and that worked for a while until her legs gave out and she started to fall and her helper couldn't easily pick her up.

Inevitably, the time came when she had to move into a home, and not just to any floor of the home, but to the third floor, full of people like her, those a little confused or very confused, a little lost or utterly bewildered.

The home was a good one with workers who cared, with sing-songs and games. But it was hard for us to adjust. Hard to sit on the edge of her bed or in the lobby and search for things to say.

And then, somehow, we decided that we had to eat together again. Dementia wards have party rooms, even if they aren't used much. And now we discovered a way to benefit from them.

Some Sundays when it was my turn to provide the food, I started early in the morning, say with something simple like a beet borscht. A pot roast pretty well cooked itself. An apple pie took a little longer, but if I had the filling prepared ahead of time and the pie crust in the fridge ready to roll out, it was not too bad at all.

All of us congregated around five at the nursing home. Snaige was always there first, getting her mother ready — few or many came now: any of her grandchildren who were around and her daughter-in law, a family friend. I carried the steaming bins inside and the regular staff who knew us asked what we were eating this time.

We wheeled my mother-in-law down to the party room and her grandchildren helped to set the place up. She was not much of a talker anymore but she was a good listener, beaming at the table, repeating how delicious the food was, and often holding the hand of one person or another. It was hard to find the words to finish a sentence, but easy to show her love with the squeeze of a hand. Her grandchildren didn't mind her at all — they sometimes served her a spoon of dessert or helped wipe the crumbs from her lap.

Some dementia ward patients can sense a party going on. Sometimes Monika came down with her walker and waited by the party room door until we opened it. She seemed to like the vibe. Aldona was steady on her feet but she couldn't speak at all anymore. She came in and sat down, her hands on her lap. She sometimes liked to take things away, a spoon or a plate, like a kind of souvenir, but she would give it up if you asked her.

And so we dined on for three years in the dementia ward, all too conscious that this wouldn't last forever. Every dinner might be the last one. Every meeting, even at the best of times, involved a calculation of that week's losses — another level of immobility, another few words of vocabulary disappearing.

This was dinner in the dementia ward, a little sad and wonderful at the same time. These meals were just shadows of our dinners of the past, just crumbs compared to the feasts we used to have, but they were still very, very sweet, and the taste of them lingered all week long.

THE THREE FACES *of* GOD

I grew up on the edge of Toronto in the fifties, in the no-man's land between the city and the country, in a working-class suburb whose religious model resembled that of a feudal village. We may have lived in a universe that include Westinghouse, Jackie Gleason, and Chrysler, but the Enlightenment was still far off.

My father set the religious tone in our house — kitsch Catholic, including Saint Christopher magnets for the Pontiac (to prevent horrible highway death), crucifixes in most rooms, and cloth scapulars for the neck. We had a variety of rosaries, from the ebony beads of my father to the shine-in-the-dark variety that I laid on pillows in dark rooms, the better to impress my Protestant friends with the superiority of the One Holy Catholic Apostolic Church.

Although my father was a strict Catholic, his views were not entirely orthodox. He believed in the New Testament, but thought the Old Testament was primitive science-fiction crap. He believed you burned in hell forever for any one of a variety of infractions, including missing church on Sunday, letting meat cross your lips on Friday, failing to genuflect when passing before the tabernacle in a church, or disobeying your husband. ·

I went to kindergarten in a Catholic convent housed in a decrepit mansion, where the black-clad nuns seemed to float noiselessly up and down the many stairs. I arrived early one grey winter morning to play with a jigsaw puzzle. The nuns were early practitioners of energy conservation, so no lamps came on before a quarter to nine. I was struggling in the weak light with a devilishly difficult Three Little Pigs cutout when I realized I was being watched. I looked up to see a nun standing in the corner. I was startled, but only slightly. Nuns were allied with God and they moved in mysterious ways. For all I knew, this particular nun who watched me so attentively might have just appeared. Or been there all night, or been standing there since the dawn of time. Like God, nuns were omniscient.

And this omniscience was terrifying, for God, like my father, had an opinion on things and He was always ready to judge. I had no problems with the other ever-present heavenly companion, the guardian angel, for by definition the angel was gentle, like my mother. The guardian angel might sigh. The guardian angel might be disappointed and wish I had lived up to my better self. But a guardian angel never really became cross.

God did. How angry could the Supreme Being be with a kid? Angry enough. He could get annoyed with me. He could get irritated easily, like my father, when he was hungover. This God was a stickler for all the rules, the small rules. He was like the punctilious hall monitors at the elementary school I went to after kindergarten. The hall monitors made sure we walked silently in neat lines on the right side of the corridor; they snitched on us for drinking at the water fountain when we were allowed to go to the bathroom only to accommodate the necessary bodily functions of urination and defecation, not to indulge trivial thirst.

In my child's universe, God the Monitor was everywhere. He snorted in exasperation when I climbed the branches of a neighbour's tree. He slapped a thick wooden ruler against the palms of His hands when we ate the butter tarts that had been stolen by more wicked friends.

"Hey, you!" God shouted when we stepped on a newly seeded lawn.

"How many times do I have to tell you to close the fridge door?"

"Just look at the mud on those shoes, young man! Do you know how much new shoes cost?"

God the Monitor watched my every childhood move with the same devotion He had employed to create the world. He scrutinized me, and I felt helpless under His relentless gaze.

This nit-picking God is more or less gone now. He walked away from me one afternoon, with a dismissive wave of His hand.

The incident had to do with a very cute girl just a little younger than me. I had asked her to come behind the garage so I could examine her for early signs of polio. This very thorough examination, which later brought down on me her mother's fury, my father's anger, and my mother's disappointment, was just too much for God.

But not entirely. We were taught that there is a little bit of God in each of us, and I still see flashes of God the Monitor from time to time. I saw Him in the eyes of the East German border guard who stared at me long and hard at Checkpoint Charlie during the Cold War. I saw Him in the eyes of the postal clerk when I tried to reuse a franked stamp. I saw Him in my little kids' eyes when they smelled cigarette smoke on me.

He lurks somewhere still, ready to appear like the nun in my kindergarten classroom. Unlike the mild nun, He is exasperated, incensed, and, now that I am old enough for it, occasionally enraged.

God the Stand-Up Comic

Unlike a lot of lapsed Catholics, I have no personal bitterness or anger at the Roman Catholic Church, although I was scandalized like everyone else at various revelations of abuse in decades past. As time goes by, I have even come to love the church again. I look back on my traditional Catholicism with fondness and amusement, for it was really very funny. Most religions are, but let me consider Catholicism for a moment.

Take the rosary.

In the sixties, when everyone else was talking free love, Toronto's Exhibition Stadium was filled with thousands of Catholics clacking rosaries in their hands. It was a hot Sunday in June when the agnostics were tending gardens and the kids were swinging in parks, feeling the delicious spring air swish by their faces. But not us Catholics. We were dressed in our jackets and ties, hats and gloves for women, and even winter coats, *just in case it gets cold down there by the lake.* Thousands of us went to church first, or were made to go by our parents. And then we were forced to go on directly, after Mass, to another religious celebration: a mass recitation of the rosary.

Of course, the concession stands were closed. A hot dog or

some popcorn would have given some comfort, but we were out of luck. It was one of those days when we felt cursed to have been born Catholics.

Down below us in the stadium, there were parish marching bands and banners with various saints on them. In the hot spring afternoon, young Catholic men down on the field fainted with some regularity as they stood to attention with those banners. We could see the collapsing standard bearers for Saint Jude's and Our Lady of the Airways. Like soldiers in battle, their comrades quickly stepped forward to seize the standards, soldiers for Christ forging forward.

In the centre of the field stood fifty-nine girls in red dresses, all arranged in the shape of a rosary, and beside each red-dressed girl stood two others dressed in white. As the thousands in the stands finished a Hail Mary of one of the beads of the rosary, the attending girls would fan out the skirt of the girl in red, and the giant rosary on the field blossomed before our very eyes. It was like an NFL half-time show with a religious twist.

A lot of my friends are entertained when I tell stories about my Catholic childhood, but mine is not the only funny religion. Most religions are pretty amusing, including new ones that don't identify themselves as religions at all.

First comes a loose collection that believes the whole project of Western civilization has been a sad mistake. Skyscrapers, cars, expressways, microwaves, and online shopping all came about because a few farmers had the wrong idea and gave up their hunter-gatherer pasts. The Bible didn't help, with its "go forth and multiply." That instruction worked all too well, like a computer virus. These people love nature, often from urban distance, but when they do go out into it, they will invest in Gore-Tex, Kevlar, mountain bikes, and ChapStick.

Another new God has been found by my business friends. These are hardheaded types, bottom-line men and women who pride themselves on their shrewdness. They scorn organized religion as they do opera houses, grants to artists, and socialized medicine. These business people have found a new god, and invariably it lies within their own hearts. They really are gods themselves, these captains of finance, and they only need to access the power within themselves to exercise their omnipotence.

I have friends who think health is God. They are fit-for-life vegetarians or evolving vegans. I was once invited to a healthy dinner of corn and pea pie in white sauce. It was disgusting. And this was some years ago. Now, no hardcore health enthusiast would offer me either wheat or dairy. Even corn has become suspect. I guess we'll be munching on kale, the vegetable kingdom's closest approximation to shoe leather.

The source of humour in many new spiritual beliefs lies in their fuzziness. They scorn all traditional religions. They say: the God of religion is dead. In the next breath, they something like, "May the Force be with you." Why is it easier to believe in the Force than in Yahweh? Or to put it another way, who needs new jokes when we haven't exhausted the old ones?

I have come back to my Catholic roots, as some Catholics do. I have some residual fear that I am blaspheming in these reflections. I am not so concerned about what people think as I wonder about what goes through God's mind as He reads these words. I remember what the late poet Czesław Milosz said about the old Catholic belief that one committed a mortal sin by missing Mass on Sunday. Who knows, Milosz mused, maybe it's true. Maybe God has a sense of humour.

God the Holy Ghost

For most of my adult life, I have not thought much about God or religion. I imagined I would come to them suddenly if a sober-faced doctor ever gave me the bad news. Alternatively, I would come to them eventually, as old people do. Now that I am at the beginning of that phase, God is starting to show Himself, elusively, in fleeting moments like a ghost. Contrary to what Wordsworth wrote, I see more celestial light as I grow older and the mystery of it keeps growing and growing.

Take the rosary, that dear old relic of kitsch. I remember the priest preaching against it in the seventies, when it seemed guitar music was hipper than stale old Johann Sebastian Bach. The habit of saying the rosary has pretty much died off in most places but when old-time Lithuanians die, the mourning family sometimes still has the priest say the rosary at the open casket. As I move into my own old age, the funerals of my parents' generation have mostly ended. But I recall one such funeral from the late nineties. When the priest took out the rosary and we were invited to kneel, I remembered only the intense religious boredom of my childhood. But I was a child no more.

The posture on my knees was mildly uncomfortable and I was a little too hot because I had not bothered to take off my winter coat in that funeral home. The repetition of the Hail Marys and Our Fathers put me into a kind of meditative trance. Much to my own surprise, somewhere in this quiet place behind the drone of prayers, a strange shadow of God was flitting, faint and mysterious.

It was hard to find this God again. But one of the mysteries of God is that He comes unexpectedly. All writers know about those rare moments when a strange kind of grace descends, moments when the words spill out unasked, a time when the language glows with unearthly presence and the words seem etched on the page.

When I was young, I wanted religion to make sense. I wanted it to be warm, good, and rational. I wanted God to be a socialist with a human face. He would redistribute wealth in my favour after he had taken care of the downtrodden first. I would be willing to wait my turn. He would be understanding of all my transgressions. He would be kind and forgiving. But who am I to dictate the characteristics of the numinous? By its very nature, the divine is mysterious. Like the big bang, string theory, and multiple universes, God may have little to do with common sense and a tender heart.

My late mother-in-law was a woman I made fun of a great deal. She took my jokes good-naturedly. She was one of the pilgrims who travelled to the religious shrine of Medjugorje before the Yugoslav dissolution. It was said that favoured pilgrims had their rosaries turn to gold, and just such a thing, she claimed, had happened to her. Not real gold, but gold colour. While she was there, her metal beads changed. I ridiculed her mercilessly, for this to me was a sign of the worst of my childhood Catholicism. This was superstition and kitsch.

But I've come around. Who am I to say God should have good taste? Who am I to say God should feed the hungry instead of wasting His time changing the colour of beads? The divine plan, whatever it may be, is mysterious, unknowable, awful. The glimpses of the divine we have are partial, terrible, inspiring, and frightening at the same time.

God lurks in the shadows, sometimes a friend but sometimes other, not necessarily with the warmth and kindness I long for. His favour is a double-edged sword. If I ever decided to ride, He might throw me off my horse, as He did Saul. He might mug me in the desert, as He did Moses.

Or He might do nothing at all.

WHERE I'M COMING *from.* WHERE I'M GOING TO

For the fourth year in a row I was standing at the crossroads of Pylimo and Traku streets in Vilnius, Lithuania, worrying the place, trying to sift the stories that lay like dust between the cobblestones. I was slightly sick of this baroque, labyrinthine city — the strangulated cries of the swallows at dusk made me think of the dead souls of forgotten citizens.

Almost nobody who lives in Vilnius now had great grand-parents who lived here — most of the old inhabitants were killed during the war or shipped out after it. Vilnius is old, but the people who inhabit it are relatively new to this city.

They came here after the war, around the time I was born to immigrant parents in Toronto. Although I had spent my whole life in Canada, my clan, my people, were new to it and I was not entirely comfortable in the country of my birth. I kept coming back to this melancholy city, mulling over the past and trying to determine the geography of belonging.

The Canadian part of my life lay neglected. I had never been to Newfoundland or anywhere truly north. I once had fantasies of drinking my way through the Okanagan Valley or of searching out whatever commercial fishermen remained on the Great Lakes in order to ship out with them. These

212

were oversights I might never remedy, fantasies I would never realize.

Much as I would have liked to write about the place where I lived, I kept writing instead about the place my parents came from.

Immigrants in the fifties were called "Displaced Persons," or DPs for short. I was undergoing some sort of reverse DP process, being pushed back in time and space.

Someone my age, nearing retirement, should have had a clearer view of his place in the world, but the complicated strands of history were getting more tangled as I grew older.

So why this ongoing return to Lithuania, a land of rolling green hills so similar to Southern Ontario? For one thing, the stories here in the old country were more brutal, the stakes so much higher than back in Canada. Placed beside the gulag, suburban angst is pitiful. And then there was the fact that my family history kept appearing in unexpected places.

I had just come from a meeting with Bernardas Gailius, a young historian who had written a magazine story about my uncle, Pranas, a man who had died in 1952, the year before I was born. My late parents remembered him as the family joker, the must-have guest at any party.

They never mentioned that Pranas strangled his lover in 1929, hid her body in a sewer, and hoped to dissolve her remains with acid from a laboratory where he and his cohorts were making a bomb to overthrow the Lithuanian president.

Such a dark story! My uncle was a murderer. Did I carry his blood in my veins?

And there were some oddities to his story — Pranas only got three years for the crime. (Extenuating circumstances? What could those possibly have been?) Part of his sentence was to support his son by the murdered lover. Somewhere I may have a cousin whose mother was murdered by our common relative.

To make matters worse, the man pictured in the magazine article photo as Pranas seemed to bear an uncanny resemblance to his brother, my father. I stared long and hard at that photo until I realized I was not just seeing family resemblance, I was looking at a photo of my father.

The photograph of the murderer was a photograph of my father.

I'd just met with the historian to ask if my father had actually been the murderer, but the historian said no. There had been an error at the magazine and they had inserted my father's prison photo by mistake. This new information was a troubling new revelation. On the one hand, my father was not the murderer. That was a relief.

But his *prison* photo?

It turns out my father had been imprisoned for being part of the same cabal of political rebels who had wanted to overthrow the authoritarian president of Lithuania.

I hadn't heard any of this before.

It made me wonder what else I didn't know about my deceased parents' lives. I would have to spend some time in the archives if I wanted to find out, because there was no one left with living memory of those events.

I was in no rush to get to those particular archives. Most people no longer believe that the sins of the fathers are visited on the sons, nor the sins of the uncles visited upon the nephews, but still one hopes for a little glory in the past, or at least a little righteousness. I was shaken.

Rather than go back along Pylimo Street to the archives, I could go forward to the Jewish museum.

If my "bad" uncle Pranas had been a shock to find out about, a skeleton whose bones would continue to rattle, I preferred to investigate the past of my other uncle, the one I was named after.

During the Nazi occupation of Lithuania, he had hidden some Jewish boys in his house. The Holocaust was particularly brutal in Lithuania, where the vast majority of local and even fleeing Jews from elsewhere were killed by Nazis and local collaborators.

At least three of the children my uncle sheltered survived the war. His widow, my aunt, still had a letter of thanks from one of their fathers. I kept a copy of this letter as a kind of talisman, a good luck charm against the horror of the past.

Thus if I went one way on Pylimo Street, I could look into the dark past of the first uncle. If I went the other way, I could look into the story of at least one decent person. I needed to settle some kind of issue of good and evil, if any such settlement is ever possible.

But because I was standing at a crossroads, there were two other ways I could also go.

If I headed up from Traku Street toward Basanavičius Street, I would end where I was staying, with close friends of my wife's family. They were Saulius and Silva Sondeckis, she a cellist trained by Mstislav Rostropovich and he the most prominent chamber music orchestra conductor in the former Soviet Union and then independent Lithuania.

They were both master storytellers, so as we sat and sipped tea and ate home-churned butter and white Lithuanian cheese, Saulius described the dark era of the 1950s, especially during the rule of Joseph Stalin, when everyone lived in fear. His stories sometimes had tragicomic or surreal spins to them. In 1960, the leader of the Lithuanian Communist Party, Antanas Šniečkus, attended a New Year's concert in the former Vilnius Cathedral, which had been first sacked and then turned into a picture gallery in 1956. Šniečkus was such a fierce communist that his own parents had fled before he returned to Lithuania with the Soviets in 1944. Saulius played George Frideric Handel's passacaglia, a piece I was unfamiliar with. Silva explained that this was originally a seventeenth-century Spanish musical form.

The cathedral was a very big space, one fraught with painful history, and the music was passionate. Once Saulius had finished playing, Lithuania's chief communist stood up and said, "Now that's what I call communist music!" No one dared to question the musical assessment of this plenipotentiary.

The chamber orchestra was very fine, soon to have worldwide renown, and it grew in stature throughout Europe, Asia, and North America. Once, an East German concert was held in near-darkness because it was attended by international communist subversives whose identities had to be kept secret.

I imagined Che Guevara in the dark hall, storing up some culture before heading into the Bolivian jungles to meet his death. And Saulius was there in his tails, his baton leading the orchestra. The frisson of politics and culture was extraordinary.

These were the sorts of stories that have pulled me back more often to Lithuania. The stories compelled me but they unmoored me as well. Canada was the haven my parents found after the war, yet I didn't feel anchored there. If my parents were cast upon a safe shore after the tempest of World War II, I sat on the beach my entire life, wondering about their loss. At times, I set out to sea in my imagination and drifted, living in neither one land nor the other. At times I felt as if I might drift away forever.

But if I have described three routes available to me at the crossroads in 2009, each of them into the past, I have not yet described the fourth route, down Traku Street into the heart of old Vilnius. I walked past the ancient mansion of the Tiškevičius family, whose portico roof was held up by a pair of titans in plaster, and descended into the maze of streets in this uneasy city.

Not far from the Dawn Gate, where a miraculous painting of the Virgin Mary is adored by pilgrims on their knees, I found a bearded young man with a cigarette between his lips and a sleeve tattoo covering his left arm. He looked a little tired, but otherwise well, this son of mine whom I had not seen for three months, since he had shipped out of Val Cartier to deploy with the Canadian Army in Afghanistan.

My relief at the sight of him was acute. He was on leave, only halfway through his tour of duty, which involved carrying a grenade launcher as a corporal in a battle group. He laughed a little as I embraced him and we went into a café to catch up. There we drank Scotch and beer, talked of the ever-present ringing in his ears and a couple of close calls I swore I would not describe to his mother until he returned from his tour of duty. At the time, I used the word "until," but I hovered over the word "unless."

His choice was not one we wanted him to make, but we found ourselves impotent in the face of his decision to delay his education at McGill. And so I stood helpless before the face of history that was playing out in front of me, much as it had played out for my uncles, good and bad, and for my hosts in Vilnius, the Sondeckis family.

A new story was unfolding for me now, with stakes just as high as those from the stories in the past. And the effect of this story was to consider my mooring in Canada.

If my son were to die in battle, he wanted his ashes to lie in a military cemetery in Ottawa. My other son would likely be buried in Canada too when his time came.

This is not all that unusual, to have one's children rather than one's parents determine homeland. It happened to immigrant families all the time. Maybe it just took a little longer than we ever imagined, one more generation than we thought.

Late in my life, I have became a fatalist. The currents of history keep on pulling us in various directions regardless of our puny desires. And history isn't just the past. History is happening right now.

※

And history keeps on happening. The problem of belonging continues to be slippery seven years after that meeting in Vilnius.

Unlike a few of his unlucky comrades in arms, my Canadian soldier in Afghanistan finished his tour, returned to Canada, and completed his studies, and then moved to live in Vilnius. So now I continue to be pulled toward that city where my parents were married and one son lives with his family. The question not only of *how* should I live but *where* should I live continues to haunt me as I stand on the doorstep of retirement. I have a grandson in Vilnius and his parents as well, so it would be natural for me to "return" there too. This, after all, had been the dream of my parents for a decade or two after World War II, at least until they gave up hope of liberation from the Soviet Union, grew old, and found their own children and grandchildren fixed in Canada.

I have another son who lives his life less dramatically, but with intense purpose, in Toronto. This son is firmly established here. He can speak the language of his grandparents but he is not fixated on the past and, anyway, Lithuania is not a particularly gay-friendly place — better than Russia but worse than Canada. Optimists say that Eastern European countries are coming along and that the situation for gays will improve in the future. But my gay son lives in the present, and that present is firmly Canadian. He dreams of the future he has in Toronto, where he is creating his adult life.

Generations wander. Children cut their roots and fly away, for the history of humanity, we know, has been one of migration. But which route is the one to take? I am perpetually at the crossroads, both in the past and in the present, a wanderer, unsure which way to go.

AFTERWORD

Some of these essays have appeared in different places, often in different forms. No essay appears here as it was originally written. "The Beer Barrel Polka" appeared in *Rampike*; parts of "Literature on the Installment Plan" in *Books in Canada*; "Town and Country" in *Cottage Life*, *Reader's Digest*, and the *Globe and Mail*; "Dinner with the Demented" in the *Globe and Mail*; "The Three Faces of God" in *Holy Writ*, edited by K.D. Miller and published by the Porcupine's Quill; "Where I'm Coming from, Where I'm Going To" in *Queen's Quarterly*.

I have dedicated this book to my wife, Snaige, and to publisher Jack David because they are the ones who made me write it. We were sitting at a bar in Windsor during Bookfest, and as always happened to me after two cocktails or two cups of coffee, I started to tell stories, primarily anecdotes I found amusing. Jack held up his hand and told me to stop talking and start writing. I sought gravitas in literature and they told me to lighten up. The two of them ganged up on me, in spite of my reservations about confessional writing.

Anne McDermid and her associate Monica Pacheco have been shepherding me through literary life for some time. I am grateful to them both. Editorial surgeon Susan Renouf cut again and again, and then healed the rest, and Jen Knoch made some brilliant observations right at the end. My writing pals and dinner companions Joe Kertes and Wayson Choy have bucked me up when I needed that. A whole army of colleagues in the School of Creative and Performing Arts at Humber College supported me again and again.

Granting agencies have been generous to me over the years. Thanks to the Ontario Arts Council, in particular Works in Progress, and the Canada Council for the Arts.

Thanks to all the people who were part of the cavalcade of my life and who appear in this book, although some of them have been masked by having their names changed. In particular, I am appreciative of my family: my wife, sons, and brothers, who appear in these pages in forms they might not necessarily recognize. One of them once said to me that he was going to write his own book and call it *The Truth*.

So how true is this book? My late cottage neighbour, Keith, once consoled me on my cottage building disasters when he said carpentry was not an exact science. Neither is memoir. What you read here is what I remember in the shape I remember it, not necessarily in the shape that a historian might create. As to dates, they are circa rather than precise. When I wrote a collection of stories inspired by childhood memories, some people told me it must be memoir, not fiction. Now that I have approached the material of my life in memoir, I expect to be accused of making it all up.

Throughout the decades, I have found that life is not "one damned thing after another." A lot of it is funny, and some of it is sad, and sometimes the two lie in very close proximity. But not always, and therefore the last quarter of the book is sometimes melancholy.

Wherever and whenever I have been, I have tried to catch the flavour of the moment, and I keep trying to get that right in spite of the clichés and the myopia about the past in popular culture. The Weston of my childhood bears no resemblance to the fifties I see on TV. The excitement we all felt as the tyrannical regimes of Eastern Europe collapsed now seems hard to grasp in the current refugee crisis and alarming political developments in that region. But it's too easy to be cynical about the joys or fears of the past in light of present knowledge. To contemporary blockheads, the past is full of cynics, criminals, and insensitive fools while we in the present strive toward perfectibility. But we'll all look like fools in the future. Some of us are fools even now.

© LIUDAS MASYS

ANTANAS SILEIKA is the author of four books of fiction. His first collection of stories, *Buying on Time*, was shortlisted for the Leacock Medal for Humour and the City of Toronto Book Award as well as being serialized on CBC Radio's *Between the Covers*. His *Woman in Bronze* and *Underground* were listed among the 100 books of the year by the *Globe and Mail*, and the latter has been optioned for a film. Antanas is the former director of the Humber School for Writers.